# CONTENTS

# DIALOGUES FOR THERAPISTS

## DYNAMICS OF LEARNING AND SUPERVISION

---

# CHAPTER 1

# PURPOSE AND
# GOALS OF
# THE SEMINAR

In these days of community mental health, a question can well be raised about the place of individual psychotherapy or counseling in a training program for psychologists, psychiatrists, counselors, or others who are about to enter one of the mental health professions. An important reason for including a great deal of supervision of individual therapy in such training programs lies in the signifi-

cant and relatively simple opportunities that this activity provides for developing self-awareness on the part of the trainee in
a situation of participant observation. Of course, no such situation is really simple, but the dyad is less complex than the
group and the community. Whether the trainees later become
administrators, group leaders, community workers, researchers,
teachers, or individual psychotherapists, the ability to be aware
of their own processes in interaction with others will not only
enrich their working lives, but will help them to avoid the kind
of defensive maneuver that temporarily alleviates anxiety but
does not augment the health or happiness of the target population.

One may ask, however, whether this training in self-
awareness could not be better developed in a therapeutic situation, either individual or group, than in a seminar. In our
opinion psychotherapy should be recommended but not required in the training of clinical psychologists and others in the
mental health field. It does not take the place of the kind of
seminar on which this book is based. Several of the students in
the seminar had already profited from intensive psychotherapy.
Several others were moved by the seminar to undertake it. But a
requirement would result, as most requirements do, in "sitting
it out" without the vital participation essential for change.

The main point to be made about this seminar is that its
primary task was to enable students to be more useful to their
clients, not to enable them to solve their own personal problems
or to promote their own personal growth. To be sure, individuals often reported that light was shed on their personal lives
through the seminar discussions. This is analogous to a lawyer's
gaining useful and interesting knowledge about internal medicine when he is engaged in litigation involving copyrights of
publications in that field. The lawyer's gain in interesting and
useful knowledge about internal medicine is neither the purpose
nor the center of his work with and for his client. In the same
way the educational work of the seminar was clearly distin-
guished from the work of therapy, in which the primary task is
to solve or alleviate or understand the personal problems of the
therapy recipients. One of the tenets of the seminar, not always

so obvious as it might seem, was that the therapist should attempt during his or her sessions with the client to be there for the sake of the client, not for himself. What he gains for himself, with the client as in the seminar, must be a by-product.

In order to be "fully present" for the client, to use Martin Buber's term, it is necessary to clear away the fears and preoccupations, the blind spots and the prejudices, with which beginning therapists, as well as more experienced ones, are heavily burdened. This cannot well be done by exhortation or by suppression or by purely cognitive learning. It can be done only through the light of increased self-awareness. In this sense the seminar was therapeutic in its intent, for self-awareness is the goal of many psychotherapies.

The experience of some students who had satisfactorily completed a personal psychoanalysis is interesting in this regard. If anyone needed proof that learning in this field can never be completed, it could be had by observing such students over the years in seminars of this kind. When they entered into a therapeutic relationship with clients, the same fears and blind spots occurred with them as with other students. Usually, however, they became aware of them more quickly.

Although the students' heightened awareness was not in itself the primary goal of this seminar, it is surely a necessary condition for optimal functioning as a therapist. In this seminar it was a means to the end of becoming useful to clients. What it may have become in the lives of individual students is another matter. In order to achieve this necessary condition, both the students and the instructor had to undergo psychic change. They had to be willing to do that most arduous of all psychological work: to face unpleasantness, evil, and even terror as part and parcel of their own make-up. One student in a more recent seminar than the one on which this book is based put it ruefully, "I always thought I was a pretty nice guy until I got in here. I didn't know I was potentially a murderer, a crook, and a coward." If students do not know that they are potentially murderers, crooks, and cowards, they cannot deal therapeutically with these potentialities or actualities in their clients.

But how is one to bring about this knowledge in

"healthy, clean" young people without bringing about at the same time debasement and self-hatred? This question is not to be answered lightly. A seminar like this cannot be taught without risk. On some students it may have little to no effect. For others it may result in a significant loss in self-esteem. But where there is no risk there is also no significant gain, and the gains for most of the students have been considerable. All eight students on whom this book is based are among those who found the undertaking worth the pain involved.

These students had in common a profound respect for the potentialities of human beings for development in the area of the "interhuman," to use another phrase of Martin Buber. Without such respect, psychotherapy is a farce, a manipulation of people as if they were objects. With such respect, the specific techniques employed and the therapist's experience or lack of it are of secondary importance. It must be within the ken of every supervisor that students who respect their clients in this way can make what seem to be terrible technical blunders and still obtain therapeutic results. This book is not intended as research into the bases for therapeutic change on the part of the clients. But the beliefs and values of the authors have a bearing on what is written here.

It is our belief that there is a paradox at the heart of all psychological work, and indeed of all human endeavor. It is an ancient paradox to be found in all the great ways of wisdom of the world and best known to the West in the simple statement that "He that findeth his life shall lose it: and he that loseth his life for my sake shall find it" (Matthew 10:39). It is no accident that a religious document formulates an underlying tenet of our work. It has become a commonplace that the psychotherapist has taken the place of the priest in many parts of modern society. One of the factors in this "takeover" has been the corruption of the priesthood, including many of the leaders of all religious sects. The corruption has been not so much by venality as by banality. Too many priests, preachers, rabbis, and so on, have had nothing of significance to say to troubled souls. Psychotherapists, who are thought by those who consult them to make more meaningful interventions, can easily be corrupted in a similar way. They can, of course, help people "to be better adjusted," "to get along better," "to relate better," "to lower their anxiety level," "to get out their anger and other feelings." These are parts of the stock in trade of many psychotherapists who demonstrate an unhappy similarity to the ultra-respectable, dogmatic representatives of the church and other religious organizations, with their emphasis on living a well-adjusted life according to rules and outward forms. Psychological rebirth, which has been the message of all great religious teachers, and which in our opinion is the ultimate goal of psychotherapy, requires dedication on the part of both teacher and disciple to something beyond the self. For teacher and disciple, read psychotherapist and client.

The paradox lies in the learning of both clients and therapists that self-interest is not to be denied but brought into focus. Therapists must realize that they are not in the business of therapy for purely altruistic motives. Clients must realize that their "care," and especially their worries, for others obscure greed and inordinate care for their own security. They often have to be given permission, overtly or covertly, by their therapists to seek satisfactions for themselves. But if the learning stops here, self-awareness becomes self-aggrandizement, and corruption of the new priesthood has set in. The search for security and personal happiness is like the search for material wealth. There is never enough. The process of inflation in the economic sphere has a parallel in the psychological. The more one has, the more one wants, and the spiral of prices and wages continues to rise.

It has not been our experience that clients in therapy or students in seminars achieve any kind of "satori" that puts them once and for all beyond this spiral. But without some dawning realization of the fallacy of the spiral and without some profound dedication to a loss of preoccupation with one's precious self, the therapeutic process is not different from conversion to a new set of rules and regulations. With such realization and dedication, the process of learning in psychotherapy is endless and endlessly challenging.

In this seminar the purpose was learning to function

better as therapists. If the students had made perfect presentations of perfect cases, this purpose could not have been achieved. The object was to open up questions, particularly the question about elements in the relationship of which the therapist was unaware. The movement in the seminar discussion, when it was successful, was toward removing the blind spots of the presenting student and of the other seminar members. One student put it, "The question for me when I'm going to present a case is: Am I going to look good or am I going to learn something?"

The focus in the discussions excerpted here is not on the psychodynamics of the clients but on the learning of therapists. Occasionally a sudden "Aha experience" occurred. More often there was a gradual realization of some facet or facets of the client-therapist relationship that had previously been hidden. Sometimes the real learning took place after the seminar was over, either in a discussion among fellow students or in the rumination of one student by himself or in an individual supervisory session with the instructor.

The learning in the seminar occurred in the difficult but rewarding situation of group interaction. In each seminar session the spotlight was on the presenting student and what he or she was learning and struggling with. But it is clear that the learning was not limited to this one person. It is also clear that the group interaction was an important part of the process, sometimes furthering, sometimes interfering, with the learning. In the commentary in each chapter attention is often called to the interactive process. Individual learning was the central concern of the seminar, as it is of this book. It was and is, however, part of the learning to see the operation of social forces even in that very personal process called individual psychotherapy.

# CHAPTER 2

THE SEMINAR
BEGINS:
METHODS AND
GROUNDWORK

The seminar members assembled for their first session with curiosity and with some hesitation. The eight students involved had heard "war stories" from their predecessors. They would now find out for themselves what it was like. The instructor began the session by introducing the idea of taping the seminars as a basis for future publication by two of the seminar members and herself. The group agreed that this could be permitted as long as the material used would be disguised to maintain confidentiality for clients and anonymity for themselves. The tape recorder was turned on and a general discussion ensued. Most of the members and the instructor already knew each other from having worked in the same graduate department.

**Instructor:**   You have all had some experience in doing therapy and in presenting cases, so that I don't need to go into detail about initial interviews, history taking, and all that. You will generally present your cases in rotation. The differences in your various backgrounds should prove an enrichment to the seminar. Some of you have had chiefly behavioral training. Some of you have come with a Rogerian approach. Some are more psychoanalytically oriented. You know that the last is more or less my orientation, though I think I have learned something from other schools of thought as well. I am not going to teach any particular theoretical orientation. My aim will be to help you to get in touch with the covert processes that are always going on between a therapist and his client no matter what the theoretical orientation may be. I trust that your aims are consonant with mine.

**Harriet:**   Do you think that the psychodynamicists and the behaviorists will ever become reconciled?

**Instructor:**   I think the techniques are separate. Desensitization, for example, simply is different from psychoanalysis, even though they might both end up with the client free of his fear of high places. It's an enrichment to have more than one technique available to clients. Suppose a client comes in who has a fear of elevators, and he has a chance at an excellent job on the 22nd floor if he can get ready for it in a few weeks. Why not try desensitization? If it works, even for a little while, it will get him over a hurdle in his living. If he wants to understand more about himself, that is another matter, and it will probably take him a longer time. I sometimes say to clients who come to me for therapy, "I don't know whether you will be happier or not, but I think I can help you to understand yourself better."

**Harriet:** You're saying the techniques are separate, but what about the theories?

**Instructor:** They seem to be very different, too. But I think the operant people have taught me a great deal in one important underlying question that they raise, namely, "What is maintaining behavior in a client that seems to be ineffective, self-defeating, and altogether stupid?" Something has to be keeping it up. We may understand its genesis on the basis of psychoanalytic formulations, but it seems to me the only explanation the analysts offer for the continued maintenance of many behavior patterns is the repetition compulsion. And that is a fine word that I believe covers over ignorance of what is going on. I'm not sure that operant conditioning explains what is going on either. But at least the question is urgently raised in our minds and we can raise it in our clients' minds. And that often turns out to be a very therapeutic maneuver, especially for clients who say they understand why they do something but still do it. You can push them then to realize that they are not noticing what is happening in the here and now when they engage in the particular behavior—for example, yelling at their children. The very fact of noticing then helps them to stop it. You can say something like, "What is making you do it again and again, since you say you understand? Try to notice it just as you begin to do it."

**Bob:** Could you say something about what the goals of psychodynamic therapy should be? If a client comes in and wants to lose weight or get rid of a stutter through a behavioral program, it's easy to see the goal. But in psychodynamic therapy it's harder.

**Instructor:** It *is* harder and more complex. A lot has been written about this. I'll just try to see if I can say something that may be practically useful to you. When you are in a behavioral framework you talk about making a contract, and it is clear what the contract is. We don't realize that, when we are not in a behavioral framework, there is a contract implied anyway, which unfortunately is not always clear. I think that the weakness of much of the therapy that is now called "insight ther-

apy" or based on dynamic principles is a kind of fuzzy-minded-
ness as to what we are about. The weakness on the other side,
namely, of the behavior modification therapist, seems to me to
be a reluctance to recognize all of what is going on in himself
and the relevance thereof. That seems to me to be his blind
spot. If we could put together the clarity that the behavior
modification people exhibit with regard to their contracts and
the awareness of the dynamic people, I should think we would
have something better than either one separately.

Anyway, here are a few things about goals that I would
keep in mind if I were you. First, the client himself can and will
set his goals. He may want to feel less depressed, less anxious, or
less tense; that is, he wants to have less psychological pain. Or
he wants to get out of an uncomfortable relationship with a
spouse or parent or friend. He may feel that he doesn't have any
significant relationship, and he wants to get *into* one because he
is lonely. That is another kind of psychological pain. It is hard
to enumerate all the different kinds of problems that a client
may come with. But the first thing is to hear what *his* goal is.
Often it will be to get rid of something. The second thing is to
think very carefully whether you think you can help him with
this goal. I am certainly not advocating that you rush in with a
blueprint. You want the client to say what is on his mind. But
then what is it that you are agreeing to? Sometimes clients are
left with quite false ideas about the kind of magic we can perform or the kind of goals that will be achieved, or even the kind
of problem that can be dealt with. Clients may maintain ideas
like this even when the therapist has been quite explicit. But at
least we don't need to play into their unrealistic fantasies. I
think you can promise to try to help clarify and to throw light
on puzzling conflicts. I'm not sure you can promise to do more.
I always find it cheering when a client comes with a question
that, in essence, says: "Why do I, a reasonably intelligent person, do such stupid things?" He's already halfway to the solution of his problem when he can ask a question like that. Sometimes it is important to reformulate the client's goal in your
own language; that is, you have to bring it in line with your own
working hypotheses if you are going to have a collaborative rela-

tionship with the client. My working hypothesis, which I learned chiefly from Harry Stack Sullivan, is that some apparently unbearable anxiety sets in when the client moves in a certain direction. The anxiety stops him from going in that direction. He may not be at all aware of the anxiety, for he often sidesteps it so quickly it doesn't get started. He uses what we call defenses to protect himself against it. Sometimes he is very painfully aware of needing the defenses or soothing devices, such as alcohol, drugs, sex, and so on. Your job is to help him discover when and where the anxiety is and to help him live through it, so that he can go on to a way of living that seems better and richer to him and to you, especially in terms of interpersonal relationships. In the back of my head, I keep the idea that if he gets over a few hurdles in the interpersonal world he may go on to something *very* much better, namely, a lack of concern with himself altogether. But that is a long story, and I don't want to stop over it now. And I don't bother a new client with it either. I think he has to get through first grade before he can go to college.

**Harriet:** I like what you're saying. To me it means that you give the responsibility to the client as much as possible, to get himself as much involved as he can in the process. I think that he has the innate potential to be able to see the problem and to make choices that will make his living easier. I see my job as trying to help him to identify those choices.

**Doug:** I don't understand what Harriet means by saying someone has innate potential. I just find that really confusing, and I'm not convinced that anyone else understands either.

**Harriet:** Well, I feel that if you look thoroughly enough at the problem and you see that the client's behavior isn't working for his benefit, then you can pose some alternatives, and I feel that he has the ability to make those choices for himself. I can't tell someone else how to live his life, but I can get him to the point where he can make better decisions for himself, but *he* has to make them.

**Doug:** Well, I agree we have no right to take away responsibility from the client, but to say he has innate potential, that he can make objectively better decisions, well, I just don't believe there are in fact things objectively called better alternatives.

**Ellen:**  I guess I feel, too, that you're never sure how the decisions are going to work out.

**Allan:**  I really don't know what you're all talking about at this point.

**Fran:**  Probably you do the same things and just call them by different names.

**Instructor:**  That's an interesting point. Do we really do the same things but feel better by calling them different names? Harriet feels better by saying she believes in the client's innate potential, and for Doug that doesn't do anything at all; in fact, it makes him uncomfortable because it's unclear. Is that right?

**Doug:**  Yes.

**Instructor:**  But I don't know what you meant, Doug, about there not being any better alternatives.

**Doug:**  I'm just wrestling with the conceptual stuff, which I find confusing. But what objective criteria are there for deciding what is the better alternative?

**Instructor:**  If there is no better alternative to the way the client is now living, what are we in the business of therapy for? Why don't we stay home and do something really useful, like digging in the ground and raising potatoes?

**Gail:**  Well, we're trying to help individuals to change, and I think there are such things as objectively better alternatives.

**Allan:**  But what criteria do you use?

**Harriet:**  It has to do with your own values.

**Instructor:**  I think that's true. If we try to think through what we consider better or worse for our clients, I think we would find individual differences among us but also quite a bit of agreement because we all belong to the same subculture in the

United States. As long as your clients also belong to the same subculture, there is not a great deal of trouble along these lines, because they will share your values, your assumptions of what is better and what is worse. If you are dealing with other cultures, then it is well to be clear and also explicit about what your values are. Otherwise you and your client may be working at cross purposes, not only in that the client naturally nearly always resists and defends against the change that another "part" of him would welcome, but because his idea of what change would be beneficial is fundamentally different from yours.

**Doug:** That really is the advantage of behavior modification. You and the client both agree that it is better if he stops stuttering or goes on a diet or whatever the specific goal is.

**Instructor:** Yes, that's so. There is a nice clarity about the goal, and you can measure how near you come to it. The trouble about psychodynamic therapy is that the goal is a process. It is harder to think about and conceptualize. Our aim here will be to try to think about the process occurring between you and your clients. There has to be something going on between you. We hope that it is a process that allows the client to overcome some obstacles in his interpersonal living. Sometimes, however, the process will be standing in the client's way; that is the reason for this kind of seminar. Sometimes we shall have to look at the process going on among *us* before we can do any useful work in the interest of the client. The ultimate purpose of the seminar is to help you to be more useful to your clients, but sometimes we have to look at ourselves before we can do that. We have to wipe the mirror clean before we can see what it is reflecting.

**Gail:** But you don't mean this to be an encounter group.

**Instructor:** My view is that the work of this seminar is like walking a tightrope between a therapy group and an objective, intellectual course of study. It is more personal than the latter and less personal than the former. When I am working with a client there is always a relationship between the client and me,

so that I personally am always a part of the work. If the seminar
is to study the interaction between each therapist and his client,
then each therapist is part of the study. This involves attitudes,
feelings, and sensitivities. It requires an extraordinary degree of
honesty, which can be quite painful. This is required not only
of the therapist who is presenting but also of the other members
of the seminar. If you want a productive learning situation, you
can't say to your fellow student, "That was very nice," when
your true opinion is that it was stupid. At the same time, a certain amount of tact is necessary in dealing with one's fellows. If
you just jump down people's throats and tell them what a damn
fool thing they have just done, they seldom hear what you say,
except to know that they have been put down. That's part of
what I mean by the tightrope. We have to strike a balance and I
can't tell you where it is. I think it is the same kind of balance
you have to strike in dealing with your clients. You don't say,
"You stupid idiot, what did you do that for?" Neither do you
say, "You're so fine and lovely, I can't imagine why you feel
that people don't like you." Of course, I'm caricaturing and
talking in extremes. Another kind of extreme is to say impulsively whatever is on your mind, and the opposite extreme is
never to say anything that might be even slightly hurtful. The
task is to strike the balance both in a therapeutic relationship
and in this seminar. It's not easy, and none of us will do it perfectly, including me. We will fall over, sometimes in one direction and sometimes in another. The only guideline I can give
you is to try to be useful to your clients and to each other.

**Fran:**    I suppose we'll have clients of all different types since
we're working in a number of different agencies.

**Instructor:**    I hope you'll have a variety of clients. That's almost inevitable since no two people are the same. We will not
be concerned here with making diagnoses, which means putting
people into categories, but in looking at the particular interaction that is going on in each case between you and your
client. If it helps any, I can say briefly something about the
kinds of interaction that you may encounter and that may be
particularly troublesome.

**Carl:**    I wish you would do that.

**Instructor:**    Well, the first problem is establishing contact and finding out with whom you are talking. That also means letting some of yourself be known, particularly you in your *role* as therapist. I do *not* mean that you waste the clients' time by giving them your life history or any other irrelevant information. I mean making it clear by your attitude that you are there for a job that is in their interest, and you are there *only* for that during the time you have set aside. Since I know something about your training, I am aware that you are all pretty good at establishing contact. The problems come after that. One important thing that clients try to do to you is to turn you into parents—good parents, bad parents, the ones they wish they had had, and on and on. This is an easy seduction to fall into. Closely related to that is the tendency of many clients to make enormous demands on you of various kinds—childlike demands, sexual, intellectual, what you will. And you, as beginning therapists, may try to fill a bottomless pit or feel guilty about not doing so. Sometimes this takes the form of the client trying to put all his anxiety, all his problems, on you; and you may be tempted to take them on yourself, as if you could relieve him of them in that way. And then, when you are unable or unwilling to solve all the client's problems, you become the target of his hostilities, and that is a hard thing to handle. It often engenders quite a bit of hostility in you, which may have other sources as well. Maybe your client isn't living up to your ideal of how a good client should behave, and so he is in your doghouse. Other problems have to do with how you are going to integrate your relationship to your client with your relationship to me and to the rest of the seminar. In other words, how are you going to use your supervision? And finally, how do you deal with termination? We probably don't have to worry about that yet, but at the end of the year most of you are going away. That will force a termination that may not be optimal for your client, and you will have to deal with that. Sometimes your client himself leaves, either because external circumstances make it necessary for him to go away, or because he decides to stop therapy with or without your agreement. If it is *with* your agreement, there is no problem. But if it is *without*, then you may well be in doubt as to what you should do. It is less common that a client stays on when you think he should stop, but that could happen too. I think a very common problem with student therapists is the fear of losing a client. Well, those are some of the things I think you will probably run into, and I hope the seminar can help you with them.

The instructor has been doing most of the talking so far, in order to orient the students to the kinds of work to be expected in the seminar. In later sessions her verbal participation becomes significantly less. In her last summary of the problems she has come dangerously close to telling the students things that they could very well figure out for themselves. She is responding to the anxiety that the students feel about a new beginning. Although some of them have been in the seminar before, the group as a whole is new. Jockeying for position has started. There is some evidence of irritation with each other and of a need to lean on the instructor's experience, in order to avoid taking an independent stand. The instructor is aware that it is about time to turn the discussion back to the students.

**Instructor:**   Do you have some questions that you would like to discuss before we stop for today?

**Bob:**   I would like to ask a question for the next time. When we present our cases, how should the presentation be?

Bob illustrates the dependence that the instructor has engendered by her teaching. This is by no means always a bad thing, since students learn by being influenced by the greater and wider knowledge that their teachers want to share with them. The danger is only in allowing students to imagine that they cannot think for themselves. The instructor at this point finds it desirable to continue to give information.

**Instructor:**   If past experience is any indication, it will turn out that each presentation is different. But for guidelines, I should think you would identify your client for us, I don't mean by his or her full name—that should be kept confidential— but in general who and where he is in his life situation, what your impression of him is physically and in general demeanor, what the presenting problem is as he sees it, what you know about his history, and how *you* see the problem. Also what arrangements or, if you like the term, what contract you made with him, explicitly or implicitly. Then you would want to summarize what has been going on in the therapy. I should also like to ask you to present in such a way that you allow us to be useful to you. If you present a completely finished product, a beautiful piece of work, that will be very admirable, but we won't be of any use to you. The simplest way to say it is that if you present us with a question or a concern, we can address ourselves to it. The question may not be clearly formulated. That's all right. It will be our job, all of us together, including the one who has presented, to try to articulate the problem. Often that means that the solution finds itself. Thus, the more openly you can present, the more useful we can be to you.

**Carl:**  I'd like to ask about the tape recording. I know it was understood that we would audiotape whenever possible and, if the facilities are available, we could videotape. I know we tell the client we are taping and that the tape will be kept carefully and soon erased and that it is confidential. But what effect do you think it has?

**Instructor:**  Perhaps some of you who have done this before would like to respond to that.

    This time the instructor decides it is really time to let the students take over.

**Allan:**  I think the clients get used to it, maybe faster than we do.

**Gail:**  The hard part is not the taping, usually, but playing the tape in the seminar with everybody listening to the stupid things you have done.

**Allan:**  It's important to explain to the client that it is in his interest. He can listen to it himself if he wants to, and having your supervisor and colleagues hear it is a protection for him.

**Bob:**  It certainly emphasizes that we are students.

**Instructor:**    That has its advantages as well as its disadvantages. It is true that you may feel your student status as a weakness and the client may use it to put you down. But at the same time you don't have to pretend that you know more than you do. You are *not* experienced therapists and you don't have to pretend that you are.

**Ellen:**    It is a relief to get all that straight, I think. But I'm still with Carl. I'm wondering about the effects it has both on the clients and on us. I suppose if somebody objects strongly, we just don't do it.

**Instructor:**    Yes, I think that's right—after you've talked about it. If you have somebody who is very sensitive about the taping, you could tell him that he could turn off the machine himself at times when he feels he does not want to be recorded.

**Harriet:**    I did that once with a client and I was surprised to find that she never turned it off.

**Fran:**    We haven't discussed Gail's point that the hard part is playing the tape in here.

**Doug:**    We're all in the same boat, I guess.

**Bob:**    Oh, I don't know about that. Some people may be in bigger or better boats than other people.

**Allan:**    We don't have time to play a whole interview to the seminar, so you can always leave out the parts where you made the worst fool of yourself.

(General laughter.)

**Carl:**    You could also break the machine or forget to turn it on or forget to bring it to the seminar.

**Gail:**    The trouble is you couldn't get away with that here. Nobody would believe it was just a simple accident.

**Doug:**    But it could be—if the machine didn't work.

**Gail:**    Well, Dr. R. would raise her eyebrows and look skeptical and pretty soon you'd begin to wonder yourself if you hadn't influenced the machine not to work.

Again there is general laughter. The group is enjoying poking fun at the instructor's tendency to interpret things in a psychodynamic framework and the tension, aroused particularly by Bob's reference to potential differences in their competencies, is relieved.

**Instructor:** I know a behaviorist who says that people's telephone answering recording machines take on the personalities of their owners just as people's dogs tend to do. Some are reliable in giving messages and some forget.

**Carl:** But seriously, if the taping makes us self-conscious, it isn't going to help the client.

**Instructor:** That's true. You'll have to find out for yourselves what effect it is having, and it will probably vary from time to time and from case to case. People have argued a lot about the effects of taping, and the trouble is that if you tape you can't find out how it would be if you didn't, at least not for that same time period. I would argue that there are indeed disadvantages in taping. In my opinion, however, when you are learning, the advantages outweigh the disadvantages. Some of the main advantages come in playing the tapes over for yourselves alone, outside the seminar. I hope you will do that. Then, when you present a case, choose some typical passage or some place that is particularly problematic. I'm not asking you to bring in the parts that put you in the worst light. You will have to decide for yourselves whether the taping is helping or hindering. If it is the latter, stop.

Although the instructor has been fairly didactic here, there is no difficulty in the students' carrying the major load of the discussion from now on. These are after all very intelligent, quite mature young people who by and large can use instruction without letting it infantilize them.

**Doug:** Could we talk a little about the use of feedback in an interview with a client? I used to work only behaviorally, and I still find it very useful to think as systematically as I can about what is reinforcing the neurotic behavior. At the same time, I am now trying to use the relationship between myself and the client. So I give a lot of feedback. I find I'm doing less and less passive listening and more active responding. I use the example of the therapeutic situation to say to the client, "Maybe this is how you act in other situations too, and it gets you in trouble."

**Instructor:** Do you have any idea how you came to change?

**Doug:** I guess I became impatient. And I thought that this passive listening is really a pathological situation. Just imagine a parent and a child in that kind of situation, and the parent not giving any feedback or any kind of direction.

**Instructor:** I guess there are a lot of "feeds" that one can "give back," and I am wondering what the feedback is that you give. It will probably be easier to know that when you present a case. Feedback is a big umbrella that covers a lot of different kinds of things. Does anyone else want to comment?

**Gail:** I wish I could be as clear as Doug is on where he stands. At the moment, I think I am trying to find a style of my own, but that may not be a good word. I have had good luck making contact with people that other therapists have had difficulty with, but then after that I don't know what to do and I become passive. I think my passivity might be a cop-out for me, and I think that's what I have to work at.

**Instructor:** Would you tell the seminar something about your experience?

**Gail:** I've worked with groups, and I've done individual counseling. I guess I've had a lot of good luck making contacts with people who have character disorders.

**Instructor:** Does anyone have a reaction to this phrase *good luck*?

**Bob:** I do, but I can't put my finger on it.

**Carl:** I'd like to know what skill it is that you call good luck.

**Bob:** Yes, how you arrange it to have good luck.

**Instructor:** Well, I think this is a place where we might try to go a bit more deeply. What do you really mean when you say "good luck"?

**Gail:**   I don't know, and I wish I did. What I would like to deal with here is my confusion about it and about things like that, about what is going on with me and the client.

**Carl:**   What I think I hear—and I do this too—is that there is some good quality in yourself that you are cutting down by calling it good luck and asking us not to look at it.

**Instructor:**   Could it be that we are not to look at it because we might become envious and then try to cut Gail down?

**Carl:**   I think that's what I meant.

**Instructor:**   We might just notice that things like this will happen in the seminar. People will try to protect themselves quite unconsciously against potential attacks by others. Does someone else want to speak about his or her orientation or experience?

**Harriet:**   In our master's program we had people representing each major point of view and I found myself drawn more toward those people who represented an existential or client-centered point of view. I think of myself more as client-centered than nondirective because I don't feel you can really be nondirective. I think that, like Doug, I'm more comfortable when I am more expressive and able to give back more in the sessions.

**Fran:**   That's when I feel best, too. I know from seeing some videotape that when I become more expressive and my hands start to move, I have more to contribute. I feel better, and I've found that the client seems to get more out of it. It works best for both of us.

**Allan:**   I'd like to raise another kind of question. Do you think it's important to have been in therapy yourself when you're a clinical psychologist?

**Instructor:**   Maybe some of you who have been in therapy would like to speak to that question.

**Doug:** I was in therapy when I was very young. I went to a shrink and I had all kinds of fantasies about what he was up to, and he didn't do anything to correct them. That's one of the reasons why I don't like the passive approach. That's an advantage I've had by being on the other end of the relationship.

**Instructor:** Did you ever bring up your fantasies in your sessions with him?

**Doug:** No, it was just for a few months. I was in high school at the time. He gave me a whole bunch of tests, and I was wondering why and what was going on. He never told me anything.

**Instructor:** I think it is very much worth noting that a battery of tests can put a person off unless it is carefully prepared and carefully interpreted afterward to the client. Even then, there are often repercussions that the client keeps to himself. You can see from Doug's example how clients respond to their therapists as they have responded to other authority figures in their lives, such as parents and teachers. Since you are all young and inexperienced in this field, you may not feel like authorities, but I assure you that will not keep your clients from thinking of you as such. Of course, Doug was very young at the time, but it sounds as if he had been intimidated by his therapist. It's too bad, Doug, that you couldn't have brought up all your questions and fantasies with him.

**Doug:** Right. I never did bring them up. In fact, it was the kind of thing where I thought he would call my parents, and I didn't know what he would tell them, and I didn't like that much.

**Instructor:** Of course. You can see how closely identified you assumed your therapist was with your parents. Maybe he was, but you didn't know that; you just assumed it. It is important to remember that this kind of thing will go on with *your* clients, too. I gather you want to bring out in the open what was not brought out in your own therapy. Have you thought about why you want to do that? Maybe someone else wants to comment, too.

**Gail:**   I think I'd like to be a better therapist to my clients than Doug's was to him.

**Carl:**   And I'd guess that it bothers Doug to have his client uncomfortable and not trusting him.

**Doug:**   Well, I don't like my relationships unexplicit. I got really annoyed the other day. A client came in, and she had seen a psychiatrist, and she was saying the psychiatrist made her feel like a complete moron, that everything was her fault and stuff like that. It really set me off because I thought it was so inappropriate. It was actually feeding into the problem. What this gal needed was quite the opposite, some support, because I felt she was a victim of circumstance.

**Ellen:**   There are millions of girls like that who think they are victims.

**Allan:**   When you said she felt she was to blame and it was all her fault, it really *was* her fault that she never mentioned it to the psychiatrist.

**Doug:**   (Sounding irritated.) Okay. Do you want to blame her for that, too?

**Allan:**   No, I don't, but I don't think you can blame the psychiatrist either, if she didn't bring it out to him.

**Bob:**   I like to encourage the client to bring things out, to talk about his fantasies, and at the same time I tell him my feelings about him. I bring myself in and use my relationship to him. If it's something the client won't face, then I use confrontation. I confront him with it. I say, "Look at what you're doing to me, and maybe this is why your friends are all turned off."

**Ellen:**   Well, that's good if it works. But your client can't always take it or hear it. I was in psychoanalysis after college, and in the long run I liked it that my analyst didn't say much and let me find things out for myself. I think it's very valuable to have been on the couch. You learn a lot about yourself, and you learn that it is often better to keep your mouth shut as a therapist than to make brilliant interpretations or confrontations.

**Fran:**   But you can help people to bring things out in the open by encouraging them or saying something that lets them bring out their fantasies.

**Carl:**   While we're on that, I have a somewhat bizarre theory about fantasies that the best therapists are the ones who teach themselves to have extrasensory perception about their client's fantasies.

**Bob:**   I think that the best therapists teach themselves to become more sensitive. I don't know if that is what you mean by extrasensory perception.

**Instructor:**   Could it be that the seminar is skirting around the question of who is the best therapist here? That is no doubt a hot potato, and what is even more hot is the question of who is the worst therapist. Anyway, it is my hypothesis that the underlying issue was just that in the last little while. I'd just like to have you notice how many things go on that are not verbalized. The issue of competition can contribute to the work of the group if everyone tries to do the best he can. It may also interfere if people become too afraid of being rejected or envied. Our time is up for today. Next time we'll have a case presentation, and that will give us some concrete material to discuss.

   In this seminar, as in most groups, there was a strong competitive element. By virtue of having been accepted into a widely sought-after graduate program, these students had had to become experts in competing and succeeding in competition ever since they were in grade school or earlier. The instructor is trying to point out that this was going on even as people were overtly discussing other issues. Although it was not the primary task of the group to learn about its own processes, it was often desirable to observe what the group was doing, particularly when its processes interfered with the primary task of learning to be useful to clients. The problem in the seminar was to use the students' competition, resistance, and transference to the instructor in the service of the task of helping clients. As in the psychoanalytic or psychotherapeutic process itself, all of these phenomena can become grist to the mill as long as they do not overwhelm the participants and the seminar leader. The aim of the seminar is to transform these primitive reactions, which psychotherapists share with all human beings, into valuable learning experiences.

Students and teachers alike may find themselves reflected in the following chapters, sometimes uncomfortably so. It may help to remember that the dialogue represents excerpts that have been edited for the reader's benefit, not literal transcriptions. It may also be helpful to teachers and supervisors to remember that they are subject to the same group pressures that are influencing their students. In other words, teachers and supervisors are also competitive, resistant, and reluctant to expose their failures, incompetencies, and insecurities. It is important that they should model for their students, not so much perfection, which is impossible, but a willingness to learn from their imperfections.

─────────────────────────────────────────────

# CHAPTER 3

# IMPASSES
# AND WAYS OUT

In this chapter, four kinds of situations that tend to plague beginning therapists are presented, one in each section. These are, of course, not the only kinds of difficulty with which student therapists are concerned, but they occur frequently. The therapist seems to be stuck in an impasse from which he can find no egress. Sometimes the dilemma is posed in the form of a question by the presenting student. "I don't know what to do," says Bob in Section 3. Sometimes, as in the first, second, and fourth sections, the question has to be teased out.

## Section 1
## Parent or Therapist

One of the common difficulties that beginning therapists encounter springs from an overeagerness to be good therapists and also to make up for all the unhappinesses that their clients have suffered by trying to be better parents or siblings or lovers than the ones the clients are complaining about. This became particularly clear in the following session. Just as clients present symptoms that both tell and conceal something of their underlying conflicts, so the therapist in recounting the story of his client often reveals signs of the underlying conflicts that he is concealing from himself.

Allan is presenting a young woman who is a junior in college. She had come in ostensibly for help in making a decision about changing her vocational goal. Her original intention had been to go into nursing, but she found herself becoming interested in design and interior decorating. To pursue this latter goal, she was thinking of leaving the area to attend a school in another city. "Should I or should I not?" was her original question.

She was apparently in a terrible state of indecision, which she said was not unusual. In telling the seminar about her family background, Allan is extremely sympathetic with her situation. She has been discriminated against by both parents in favor of a younger brother who, according to her story, received all the love, all the concern and all the money that the parents could give. Allan tells in detail how she has suffered as far back as she could remember. Nothing she ever did was right. There was no communication between her and her parents. Her brother, just a few years younger, could always do everything better; he was clearly the parents' favorite. She had always been accused of being in the wrong in the fights with her brother, even when he had started them. There were many tales of neglect and loneliness. In her first two years of college she had no close friends and had relied on taking drugs with a group of classmates for a little sense of companionship. She stopped taking drugs about a year before the interview, when she found that she chose her companions indiscriminately while she was "tripping." Allan describes the drug experiences that she has been telling him about over the past three sessions. Finally he completes his presentation without any reference to the original problem.

**Carl:**    I was wondering why you let her go on talking about the drug experience for so long. She isn't tripping any more, is she?

**Allan:**    No, she isn't. It just seemed as if she wanted to talk about it.

**Instructor:**    Could it be that she was talking about it to avoid something more important? Do you remember how you got into it?

**Allan:**    No, I don't. Maybe it was an avoidance, but it seemed important to her to talk about the drugs. I guess I found it interesting, too, to hear about her experiences. They were not bad, just very nice while they lasted.

Allan here has a glimmer that he had been led along on an agreeable detour without questioning its significance. The scenery along the way had been interesting, and the journey had become a pleasant, comfortable interlude for him and no doubt also for the client.

**Ellen:**    The drugs aren't a problem for her at the moment, are they?

**Allan:**    No, not now.

**Gail:**    I was thinking of the first session, when she came in with the problem of deciding about a school change. What happened to that?

**Allan:**    We haven't talked about it for a while. When she first brought it up, I thought there was more involved than changing schools. She needed to find some identity or purpose for herself. I thought she needed more self-confidence.

**Carl:**    What would keep her from changing schools? It seemed like a good idea, really.

**Allan:** I'm not sure I can answer that. We haven't talked about it.

**Fran:** She thinks her parents regard her as the black sheep of the family. But I wonder if she doesn't give them a hard time, too.

**Allan:** I don't really know.

Allan has become defensive and his voice has risen sharply. None of the seminar members seem to share his sympathy for his client. Instead they are questioning critically what he is doing with her. And his intentions had been so good!

**Carl:** While you were giving the presentation, I was becoming impatient. It seemed as though the important aspects of communication were not there.

**Instructor:** I think I agree with Carl. Since the first session we haven't heard anything about what is troubling her in her present life.

**Harriet:** As Fran said, I can't tell whether it really is all her parents' fault or whether she sets it up so that they won't recognize her as a person who needs something from them.

**Allan:** They really never have supported her or helped her. They didn't listen to her when she wanted to talk to them and tell them about herself. Her brother never was interested in her, either.

**Bob:** So you would naturally want to be a better parent and a better brother to her.

**Allan:** I was just trying to understand her.

Bob has put his finger on what Allan was doing. He is going to an extreme in not wanting to be like the "bad parents." But Allan is not yet ready to see it or to look into the implications of his behavior. While trying hard to be a good "parent" and a good therapist, he is actually wasting his client's time and feeling somewhat guilty about it.

**Instructor:**  I would be interested to hear part of a tape, to get a firsthand impression of what this girl sounds like. Did you bring one?

**Allan:**  No, I don't have one.

**Instructor:**  May I ask why?

**Allan:**  After the first two sessions I didn't make tapes. I thought those first two were too far back, so I didn't bring them.

**Instructor:**  Any special reason you stopped taping?

**Allan:**  I'm not sure. I just did. Maybe for the same reason that I let her talk on and on about the drugs. I guess there's a lot of anxiety underneath.

**Instructor:**  Whose anxiety?

**Allan:**  I guess my own. I feel a little guilty about not taping. I wonder about that now.

Allan has admitted that he is uneasy and uncertain about what he has been doing with this client. He has courageously overcome his defensiveness, to some extent at least, and is willing to try to explore where he is having trouble.

**Instructor:**  Well, it really is interesting to think about. How do you suppose this happened? I think you yourself have been convinced by hearing other clients how useful it is to have a tape so that we can get a bit of the flavor of the actual back-and-forth between you and the client. You did make two tapes and then mysteriously you stopped. There are also these other things that people have been asking you about and commenting about in your presentation. Some very important data are missing. She's not talking about anything that is concerning her now. The whole presenting problem has gone underground. Do you have any idea what happened about this?

**Allan:**  I'm thinking that that really isn't where the heart of the problem lies.

**Instructor:** You may well be right about that. But we're not hearing from you where it does lie and you're not hearing it from her. I think what we're all asking you is why you are beating about the bush. You're wandering with her all over the earth and not focusing on what is the trouble. And, alas, you don't have ten years to work with her. Am I hearing the rest of you correctly that this is the way you feel, too? Speak now or forever hold your peace.

(Heads nod in agreement.)

**Allan:** Yes, you're right. I'm visualizing now our next session, and I'm thinking I'll say to her something like what you've been saying, and I could ask her for her reasons for coming to see me and also what she's thinking about changing schools.

Allan has agreed a little too quickly, without working through his difficulty with the client. It often happens that a therapist wants to make speedy use of a technique, a phrase, a question that someone has suggested to him without fully understanding why he should do this, but simply because the teacher has spoken or because a certain formulation sounds good. Allan has fallen into this trap, partly because the seminar seems to be so united in feeling that he has let the client avoid anxiety-arousing material for too long, partly because he himself knows that something is wrong.

**Instructor:** Before you practice it out, why don't you ask yourself the question that we're trying to ask you. Why do you suppose you have been letting her wander all over the lot? If you get a deeper understanding of that, then the things to say to her will come to your mind of themselves. Actually in the first session she let you in on quite a bit of trouble. She's a loner. She can't make decisions. She feels furiously angry and competitive toward her brother. She's faced with a specific decision about schools, which she has to make pretty soon. There's plenty of trouble, but where has it gone?

**Allan:** I guess Bob was right before. I feel I have to be very nice to her to make up for how mean her parents are.

Allan illustrates here a phenomenon that occurred frequently in the seminar. A point is made by someone and denied
by the presenter, but a little bit later it emerges in the latter's
mind as making a great deal of sense. This happens especially
when it is not rammed down the presenter's throat.

**Ellen:**   I thought you were feeling very, very protective toward
her.

**Fran:**   I thought you were doing everything possible to avoid
competing with her, too.

**Allan:**   I really didn't want to compete with her.

**Fran:**   If you did, you'd be like her brother.

**Allan:**   I'm not sure how her brother is.

**Fran:**   Well, he's more successful. He's already found a professional identity, even though he's younger. He's hellbent now for
medical school as you are hellbent for being a psychologist. He
knows how to please people and so do you.

**Ellen:**   I think if it were me, I'd find it safer to be protective
and kind as you have been. If you act very competent, then the
danger is that she sees you like her brother and that means competition. I wouldn't want that either.

**Instructor:**   I got the impression as you talked that you were
keeping it all very low key, very smooth, not a ripple on the
water, and that she didn't experience any anxiety or difficulty
in the sessions. Did the rest of you feel that, too?

(Heads nod.)

**Allan:**   What I'm thinking now is how to go about changing it.

Allan is still more preoccupied with what to do than with
trying to understand what has been going on within himself.

**Instructor:**   Could you just notice the rise and fall of your own
anxiety in the sessions? That will tell you a lot. But may I come
back to the matter of her presenting problem? How do you feel,
just off the top of your head, about her changing schools?

**Allan:**    I guess I'm not very keen on it.

**Instructor:**    It would mean going away from you, wouldn't it? If she decided to change schools? She'd be leaving the city.

**Allan:**    (very thoughtfully) I wonder if I'm keeping her here for me and not for her and if that's why we have avoided talking about that issue.

**Instructor:**    I thought maybe you felt a little bit glad that she had stopped talking about transferring to another school. I would think that you do want to be a better father to her than her own father, and then she wouldn't want to go away from you.

**Allan:**    Yes, and I also want to be a good therapist, and I don't want to lose her as a client. I see the bind I create for myself.

**Instructor:**    It's only a bind if you're not aware of it. If you are aware and can comment on it, even just in your own mind, it gives both you and her more freedom. But you can't comment on it unless you see it happening.

**Allan:**    I think I see what I'm doing.

**Instructor:**    As long as you don't fall over backward now and do the opposite. You don't have to be the mean father to avoid being the indulgent one.

**Allan:**    But I do need to decide when to move in.

**Instructor:**    It will help if you just notice your own anxiety level in the sessions. I don't mean you should always go head-on into the midst of it, but notice where and when you move away from trouble. It's true, there are always decisions to be made in therapy and one doesn't always make them correctly.

**Allan:**    I don't think I realized how much I felt that I needed to just keep her coming. I wanted her to like me, and I needed to have her as a client for the seminar.

Allan has now very courageously faced his own need for the client. The natural wish to be liked and the wish to keep a client in therapy are threads that run through many case presentations. For people in the mental health professions, pleasant and supportive behavior to others in trouble is often such an ingrained, well-learned habit pattern that it is difficult for them to question its appropriateness. Fortunately for the learning of the seminar, Allan had in this case carried the behavior to such an extreme that the others were moved to challenge it. Finally, he himself saw that his apparent kindness had not been in the client's interest. It had seemed to him that he ought to make a special effort not to appear unkind and to try to make up to his client for the neglect that she had apparently experienced from her parents. He felt that he ought to try to be a good father— permissive, supportive, approving, comforting. But no thera- peutic movement was occurring. The client was telling him interesting stories, continuing her complaints about her family, and not changing in any way. Allan's initial lack of anxiety in his report was a clue to his collusion with his client in avoiding important issues. To be a therapist in this situation is not the same as being an eternally tolerant parent. But neither is it the same as being a punitive parent. It requires a firm and cour- ageous confrontation of the client's conflicts. The stance re- quired of Allan as a therapist is difficult to maintain. The instructor often called it "walking a tightrope." Clients pull and tug at their therapists to approve or disapprove, reward or punish their behavior. It is difficult to learn to interpret without being cold and harsh on the one hand or uncritically accepting of defensive maneuvers on the other. At the end of the seminar session, Allan had begun to see that he did not have to be caught in the impasse of being either the kind or the cruel father to his client. His job was to be her therapist.

## Section 2
## To Give or Not To Give

Another theme that occurs in many of the presentations becomes particularly clear in the following excerpt. What does the therapist do in the face of a client's overwhelming demands for help and support? Beginning counselors have learned that they should not give advice or try to steer their clients' lives. They have also learned that they should be warm and supportive. Actually both of these nostrums play into their own wishes. They want to be good mothers and fathers to their clients, better parents than the clients have had and better than their own parents have been to them. On the other hand, they are afraid of the enormous responsibility that this entails. Even when they are intellectually aware of the conflict, they find it hard, in the individual case, to be aware of the intensity of their own ambivalence. Shall they give, or shall they withhold? In the following case the similarity of two clients finally made the way out of the impasse become apparent.

Harriet was presenting a new client, but before doing this, she had given a brief report on what had happened to another client, Helen, in whom the seminar had been very interested. Helen had been hospitalized after a suicidal attempt which, though rather carefully planned so that it would not succeed, was one of a series of dramatic calls for help. Harriet had felt this case very keenly as a failure on her part and had reported the incident in a depressed manner. Seminar members were overtly sympathetic, but there was some evidence of irritation with Harriet's depression.

She is now presenting her new patient, Nancy, in a wooden, stilted style that is different from her usual active, lively participation. Harriet has droned on for some time, giving the client's background and family history and playing part of a tape. Nancy is a seventeen-year-old college freshman.

**Harriet:** Nancy said she wanted advice on how to handle her homosexual feelings toward her roommate. Then she said she had been in therapy in high school with another woman therapist, but she had never felt free to tell her about the homosexual feelings she had experienced then toward several different classmates. She indicated that the previous therapist had been cold, but that I was warm. She felt that I could help her and understand her better.

**Fran:** Excuse me, but—Bob, the Coke I got you during the break is up there and I don't know whether you saw it.

**Instructor:** This may be a bit far out, but I wonder if that Coke bottle isn't relevant.

**Fran:**   I knew it as soon as I said it.

**Instructor:** Okay, tell what the relevance is.

**Fran:**   I don't know. I guess I was bored. I wasn't really listening.

Fran has moved away from her initial intuitive understanding of what she had done and is feeling slightly frightened at having caught herself in an act that was more meaningful than she had consciously intended it to be.

**Gail:**   I thought Harriet had given a very well organized history.

**Bob:**   I did know the Coke was there, Fran, but thanks anyway.

**Carl:**   Why didn't you bring me one?

**Ellen:**   The history was hard to get, too, since she kept trying to make you give her support and advice all the time.

The seminar members, without realizing what they are doing, are all responding impulsively in one way or another to the themes of nurturance and protection. Bob and Carl are referring to Fran's caring—or not caring—for them. Gail and Ellen are protecting Harriet, really quite unnecessarily, against what could be felt to be an attack by Fran, who had admitted to being bored. The fact is that other seminar members, too, have given signs of restlessness and boredom, but people feel that Harriet has had such a bad time over the hospitalization of her patient, Helen, that they wish to protect her and are reluctant to add to her discomfort. At the same time, they are slightly irritated because she is withholding her affect from them. They want somebody to give something, if only a Coke.

**Doug:**   Isn't she seducing you, Harriet, by saying she's sharing something with you that she wouldn't share with her other therapist?

**Ellen:**   Well, coming back to the Coke bottle, that's what she's asking for, isn't it? The bottle, or maybe the breast. She's always thinking the bottle is going to be full, and when it's not she gets very upset.

**Harriet:** Yes, she's always yearning to have her roommate come and sit beside her and pet her when she's lying in bed, but she's afraid to say it to her. Then she asks me what she should do.

**Instructor:** Shall we ask Harriet to say what she would like us to focus on in our discussion?

**Harriet:** I don't know. I decided not to ask a question, but just to say, "Here it is and you take it from here."

Here Harriet, herself, has assumed the role of the helpless, nurturance-seeking client. She presents herself as incapable of formulating the problem and simply throws the responsibility on the seminar.

**Instructor:** I think you said something earlier about feeling defensive about this client.

The instructor is trying to get into Harriet's difficulty, but she, too, is "helping" more than is actually necessary. She could have pointed out to Harriet and to the seminar the process in which they were all engaged.

**Harriet:** I think maybe I'm being defensive about mothering her, and I may be getting sucked into it anyhow. When she came in and said she needed advice, bells went off in my head; and when she said she was telling me this thing she hadn't told anyone before, bells went off again. And my defensive feelings are tied up with that.

**Instructor:** Usually when one feels defensive there's something to defend against. I don't like to put Fran on the spot, but can you say any more about your feeling bored? I think there's something important in that.

**Fran:** I know now why I was bored. I was thinking the whole time about Helen, and I couldn't concentrate on this new client.

**Ellen:** I really was, too.

**Instructor:** Well, instead of fighting it off, let's bring Helen in and talk about Helen.

**Gail:** Harriet was very mothering with Helen. We sometimes thought she was too mothering, maybe smothering, like Fran with Bob and the Coke bottle. Maybe that's why Helen had to act out. And now the same thing is going on with Nancy.

**Instructor:** What do you think, Harriet?

**Harriet:** I keep thinking of Helen, too. She's been getting in my way with other clients.

**Instructor:** How is that? I raise the question because, if you have a difficult client—and Helen certainly was—and if you live through it one way or another, usually you learn, and it helps you with others. But you feel it's not helping. You say she's getting in the way.

**Harriet:** It's better now, but for about a week, I went into all my sessions feeling bad about not making it with Helen and expecting I wouldn't make it with anybody else, either.

**Instructor:** Something of that came through to the seminar, some of your feeling of depression, so that people felt bored and didn't want to listen.

**Allan:** Where I started getting turned off while we were listening to the tape, and also a little annoyed, was when she actually told you she probably would make unmeetable demands on you. She seemed genuine and quite uneasy then. Her voice rose about two octaves. But you didn't hold her to that. You changed the subject and asked about her previous therapy, and she had sort of played games with that by not telling the other woman what she was concerned about.

**Fran:** She wasn't quite honest, was she? I was feeling a lack in your presentation of how you feel about this girl. Is that what you're defending?

**Harriet:** I think you're right on the sore point. I was really hoping you could pick it up. She was acting as if her problems didn't really trouble her all that much, and here was I, sweating about what to do for her.

**Instructor:**   What *were* you doing?

**Harriet:**   I was thinking she just wanted me for support and advice—someone to hang on to.

**Ellen:**   That was the problem with Helen. She was a terrible burden for you, Harriet, and yet when you had an opportunity earlier, to get rid of her, you didn't do it. This is the same thing, only not so dramatic and not so acute.

Harriet has now become clear about her own irritation with the client who was attempting to dump her problem on the therapist. In part she welcomes this and is happy to play the warm, nurturing mother. In part she is angry at the demands made upon her. Now that she has a client who does not arouse as much anxiety as the very disturbed Helen, she is able to grasp the situation more clearly.

**Instructor:**   I think it is the same problem fundamentally. The client says she is concerned about homosexuality or some other problem. In a way it doesn't matter what the problem is, because in each case she is trying to get you to take it on. The problem can shift from one day to the next. This is the deception she is practicing on you, and you are indeed being seduced. It's hard to hold the patient to the anxiety that that arouses. As Allan pointed out, you changed the subject when she came close to it.

**Gail:**   It's essential to hold the client's nose in it.

**Allan:**   Holding her nose in it has a punishing, distasteful tone. But I think you have to show them the deceptions.

**Instructor:**   It's not only *their* deceptions, which are usually self-deceptions. But it's holding yourself in the anxiety and not moving away to something that is nice and calm.

**Carl:**   It's easy to get confused by the stereotyped role of the therapist as a warm, supportive person. We all have trouble with that. It's a constant question for me. How do I affirmatively adopt a "no-BS" posture with a person who says he's in misery?

**Instructor:** That is exactly the difficulty. And it is often a question of timing and dosage. With this client it could be easier than with Helen, since she isn't threatening suicide and homicide and God knows what else.

**Harriet:** I *was* reluctant to stay with her anxiety in that session. I sensed that I was backing off.

**Instructor:** Well, there you have it. You've seen the crucial point. People were reluctant to point it out to you because they were taking such good care of you. The seminar was being overprotective of you, as you were of the client. That was where Fran and the Coke bottle helped us.

**Ellen:** That's happened to me, too. I've built up a lot of anxiety about pointing out something to a client. I've been actually shaking and scared of what terrible thing I might do to him, and when I get up enough courage and say it, he sits back in relief and says something like, "Thank God, you've finally said it."

**Harriet:** Yes, that's the way it was today. I was really hoping underneath that somebody would see through me and say that I was not coming out with what I was doing, and it was a relief when you all stopped being so polite and kind.

This session is a model of what could and did sometimes happen in the group when the presenter was not too defensive and the seminar neither too attacking nor too protective. The problem of dependency is one with which not only clients but also therapists themselves are often struggling in relation to the important people in their personal lives, including parents, spouses, and teachers. It is not surprising that exaggeratedly dependent demands of clients for protection and nurturance should arouse strong feelings and make it especially difficult for students to maintain a therapeutic stance. As in the preceding section, the way out consists essentially in standing still. The real question is not whether to give or not to give advice and support in answer to the client's apparent need. The real question is how and when to comment on the client's need so that he can hear and use the comment.

## Section 3
## To Run Away or To Sweat it Out

Anxiety is often an integral part of therapeutic interactions. Students, eager to do good and be helpful, are often not aware of how much gruelling anxiety is involved on the part of the therapist in therapy. They have to learn that some discomfort is part of their work, part of what they are paid to do, part of the price they must pay for the rewards in inner satisfaction, status, and money that go with this profession. In the following case, however, the question of how to maintain a therapeutic stance became especially acute. It was an advantage that the therapist did not feel the need to deny his anxiety.

The client, a 26-year-old engineer, came to the agency stating that he was unable to concentrate on his work. He illustrates a phenomenon that is fairly common, especially in student populations. Clients come for help ostensibly because of some difficulty in concentrating or studying. As rapport is established with the therapist, it turns out that the problem includes other, more emotional aspects. The therapist, Bob, describes how the client presented himself.

**Bob:**   He seemed alternately depressed and upset. Sometimes he just sat and looked down at the floor and spoke slowly. Sometimes he looked up and shot sort of pleading glances at me while he moved around in his chair. He said he used to be bothered just part of the time, but it is now getting worse and he is afraid he may lose his job.

It wasn't until the second interview that he told me that when he can't concentrate he is all the time thinking one particular thought that he can't get out of his mind. He is afraid that he has syphilis and that he will die from it. He didn't go right away for a medical checkup when the thought began to bother him, but after a while he did and all the tests were negative. He doesn't have anything wrong with him physically. Partly he believes that, but he doesn't quite, and the worry

persists. He thinks maybe they mixed up his tests with somebody else and he really does have syphilis.

I said he could go and have them done again if he thought
that. But he didn't really answer. He just said that he was getting pretty desperate and didn't know what he would do. I was
getting pretty desperate, too. I was afraid he was thinking of
suicide. The intake worker who saw him first didn't say anything about that. It seemed he was just somebody who was having a little trouble on his job. The worker knew I had counseled
with students on their study habits and thought I might use
some of those techniques with him. Well, I tried, but he just
seemed to get into more despair.

**Instructor:**    It sometimes happens that a client doesn't let on
in the initial interview how disturbed he is, especially if he
knows he is not going to go on seeing that person as a therapist.
You may have been saddled with a client who is sicker than the
intake worker thought. But let's see what you can tell us about
his history.

The instructor has seen a need to intervene, to offer some
reassurance and to allay some of the mounting anxiety. Bob
then summarizes a complicated history of his client, who had
had a lonely childhood and a troubled adolescence. He was
essentially an only child; a brother, nine years younger, was not
of much significance for him, since there was little contact between them. His father became ill when the client was ten years
old and died two years later of cancer of the spine. During his
father's illness, the client's mother had had affairs with other
men and had left her husband a few months before he died. The
client had stayed on with his father and a housekeeper until the
father's final hospitalization. After his father's death he had
gone to live with his mother, who had remarried. Since then she
had been divorced and remarried twice. The client did well in
school and had a good job working in relative isolation. Until
recently he had had little dating experience. A few months prior
to coming to the agency, however, he had met a girl who had
taken the initiative in starting and maintaining a relationship
with him. At the same time, his job had become more demand-

ing and had brought him into contact with a group of people who had to work together. It was around this time that he began to have trouble concentrating and the fear developed that he was suffering from an incurable venereal disease.

**Bob:**   I couldn't see why he should develop this idea just when he was being more successful. He had a girl who was interested in him and he was being moved up on his job. He really sucked me into his conviction that something is terribly wrong with him physically and that he is doomed to an early death. I just felt awful for him and I expressed sympathy, but I really didn't know what else to do except to get his history. I tried to find out how he felt about his father and mother but he said he had sort of blanked out the time when his father was dying. He supposed he felt sad; he liked his father. All he could say about his mother was that she was a very good-looking woman. He doesn't see her much any more since she lives a long way off. I was kind of shocked that she would leave his father just when he was dying and I guess I showed that. But he said his father was very understanding about it and didn't seem to be angry. Then he became impatient talking about all that and he came back to his fear that he is doomed. He said there was some story about a great-uncle becoming blind and dying of syphilis but he wasn't clear about it. He sometimes thinks he can't see so well any more and he says it wouldn't be worth living if he were blind. I don't know if I should try to get him to a hospital, but I don't think he would go. My next appointment with him is tomorrow—I thought maybe I would get sick myself, but I guess I saw through that. But I don't really know what to do.

**Gail:**   It's very scary when you wonder if your client is going to jump off a bridge. I know, I've gone through that.

**Doug:**   He didn't say he was going to do that.

**Gail:**   Well, that doesn't mean he won't. And you can't hold his hand 24 hours a day either.

**Instructor:**   That's true. Sometimes you just have to sweat it out. Clients do sometimes commit suicide, and it has happened to the best of therapists. It is one of our occupational hazards, to say nothing of the hazards to the client. You didn't ask him about this?

**Bob:**   No, I was just too scared. I wanted to run.

In view of Bob's anxiety, the instructor thinks it desirable to spell out some practical steps to provide Bob with alternatives and to help him stand back and view the situation a bit more matter-of-factly, so that he can begin to think about his client.

**Instructor:**   I think we might all have been scared. It usually is a good rule of thumb to stand still on such occasions. If your client is going to commit suicide, he isn't going to do it any faster if you ask him seriously whether he has thought about that and what he has thought. You can also tell him that this is a risk you are taking together and ask him to call you if he is afraid he may do it—and assure him that you will help him to get someplace where he will be protected. You can assume that if he were fully determined to commit suicide he would not be coming to see you. Also, if it continues to be a really pressing problem, then you have help in your agency. If you really want to, you can turn him over to someone else and tell him very honestly that you do not have enough experience to help him with his problem. I think that clients can appreciate that kind of honesty. But let's see first what we can make of all this, since you are going to have an interview with him tomorrow in any case. What do the rest of you think?

**Harriet:**   I keep thinking of a book I read by Martin Buber called "Between Man and Man," where he describes how his whole development was influenced by somebody who came to see him in deep distress and who afterward committed suicide. He didn't feel that he had actually been *with* him enough or he mightn't have killed himself. If that hadn't happened, Buber might not have become such a great man.

**Allan:**   Well, if I were Bob, I would rather not have my client commit suicide, even if I didn't become a great man.

**Instructor:** Fortunately, nobody is giving you this choice to make. I recommend that book by Buber, too, but right now let's try to understand this client.

**Ellen:** I don't find it so puzzling that he developed the idea of syphilis just as he was being more successful. I think he might be scared to death of getting into a relationship with a woman that might lead to marriage. He might be scared of succeeding on his job, too. Wasn't his father pretty successful just before he got sick and died?

**Bob:** Yes, that's true. But then he should have been scared that he had cancer, not syphilis.

**Ellen:** Oh, well, the unconscious is not always so logical.

**Instructor:** Not only that, but a symptom may serve more than one purpose. It looks to me as if this symptom was serving about half a dozen. That may give it some of its power.

**Harriet:** Yes, not only does it give him a reason not to have sex with this girl, but it gives him the power to do her a lot of damage, to do any woman a lot of damage.

**Doug:** Do you think he doesn't want to have sex with her?

**Bob:** I'm not sure. He talked as if he had earlier, but couldn't now because of the idea he might infect her.

**Gail:** I should think a man with his history would be scared to death to have sex with a girl, but he might not want to recognize that. Women must seem very dangerous to him, but attractive, too. The one thing he says about his mother is that she is good-looking, and obviously she doesn't have any trouble attracting men.

**Bob:** I'm remembering now that he used the word *retaliate* or *retaliation* a remarkable number of times. I was struck by it at the time, but I didn't know what to make of it.

**Allan:** Who was retaliating?

**Bob:** Well, actually nobody. He used it negatively. He said his father did not want to retaliate, and when he talked about himself and some incidents in school he spoke of not retaliating.

**Instructor:**   What do you make of that now?

**Bob:**   Well, it seems as if maybe he *did* want to retaliate, but couldn't do it or couldn't allow himself to do it.

**Instructor:**   So we might begin to hypothesize that he would feel guilty if he were to retaliate for some of the things that have been done to him, so he finds a way that he can get back at people, especially women, or at least have the power to do it without knowing it. That might be one of the sources of the symptom.

**Bob:**   Maybe I could begin to work on that with him.

Bob has already begun to think and try to understand his client and to think of a way in which he can help him. The effect of the discussion has been to get him over his mental paralysis.

**Carl:**   It will probably be hard to get him to see that he wants to retaliate. He has a model of his father who was so "understanding."

**Doug:**   Maybe you could first work on his fear of being successful on his job. Ellen was saying that he would be scared of that, too.

**Fran:**   That started when he had to work in a group and groups usually mean competition—if we can judge by this group!

**Instructor:**   But also collaboration if we can judge by today. And this man hasn't had much practice in that. He hasn't had much experience of the kind of mutual support that a group can provide to its members when it's working well.

**Bob:**   That's true. I don't feel nearly so anxious about seeing this man. Of course, I may be scared again tomorrow, when I'm in the same room with him.

**Instructor:** But now you have something to think about besides how anxious you are. You will have to decide which aspect of his problem to take up with him first. Perhaps he'll help you to decide by bringing in some material that will point in one or the other direction.

**Bob:** At least I have two ways to go. Before, I didn't feel I had any.

This session is another example of how useful the group could be when the members worked together. Collaboration was facilitated by the recognition that Bob's problem was a difficult one, that he was being honest and undefensive in dealing with it, and that it was one that they all either had faced or would face at some time. But no amount of group collaboration can completely remove the therapist from his lonely position on the firing line when a client threatens suicide or some other form of destructive behavior. He simply has to learn to "sweat it out," recognizing that he may be impotent to effect any beneficial change. Sometimes he must recognize that his own mistakes have permitted, if not encouraged, a client to continue on a destructive course. In Bob's case, no damage had been done. As a result of the session, Bob learned that there was no way to avoid anxiety in dealing with disturbed and suicidal clients but that there were ways of understanding his client's problems that could alleviate the anxiety and help them both out of the apparent impasse.

## Section 4
## Which Authority To Follow

Students who work in a setting in which their teachers have differing or even opposed theoretical views and use different therapeutic methods may understandably become confused and uncertain about which authority to follow. While, in the long run, presentation of different viewpoints is educationally enriching, in the short run it involves difficulties of which students may not be fully aware. In the following excerpt this particular difficulty had to be teased out, since it was not immediately apparent to the student therapist that this was a stumbling block for him.

The seminar had been discussing the confusion that had arisen with an eighteen-year-old female client who claimed that her reason for wanting therapy was that she must decide within the year whether or not she wanted to have children. No external circumstances were forcing such a decision. The seminar had raised a question as to whether the therapist had unwisely gone along with the client's formulation of what the therapeutic work would and could accomplish. In other words, the question had been raised as to whether the therapist, Carl, had made an appropriate contract with his client.

**Instructor:**   What would be wrong with saying what you as a therapist can and cannot do, or what you will and will not do, with this particular client?

**Carl:**   At the moment I don't know why I didn't do that, and that's what I'm sitting here wondering about. It still doesn't seem right to me—all this that we're talking about. Something isn't right.

**Instructor:**   You mean it doesn't click, doesn't make sense?

**Carl:**   Yes, well, one thing is that making contracts for specific things has been part of our training, but in a different way.

**Instructor:**   For specific things? Like what?

**Carl:**   Well, for example, you might make a contract with a client to try to increase the frequency of dating behavior.

**Gail:**   I've had problems with this, too. I think my lack of certainty about what to do with a particular client comes at the point of making a contract, of saying what we would be doing together.

**Instructor:**   So the question is, Which authority are you going to follow this time?

**Carl:**   Right, right; I had this problem before.

**Instructor:**   You had the problem before, but now it has a new element. You now have still another authority, namely, me. Is there discomfort in deciding whom to follow?

**Bob:**   It's never—well, it's never all one way. Certain things in each school make sense to me, and others don't. I guess I haven't taken a stand. I haven't decided for myself what is appropriate.

**Allan:**   I feel pulled back and forth, too.

**Instructor:**   You said you were taught that you should make a very specific contract, Carl. Did I hear you correctly?

**Carl:**   Yes, this was part of the training.

The students are talking about training they have received in behavior modification in previous courses.

**Bob:**   Yes, the client comes in with symptoms. You find out exactly what the symptoms are, and you change them.

**Doug:**   You assume the client is the best thermometer of his own temperature, so he is the only person who can tell you what his problem is. Then you set about using the techniques you know to help him change them. That is quite a lot different from what we talk about here.

**Instructor:**   Perhaps I could translate it into my language quite simply.

**Ellen:**   I get the feeling somehow, if you translated it, it would not be so simple by the time you got through.

Some members and instructor laugh. It is a relief to be able to make a joke about the difficulties they encounter in understanding and applying unfamiliar concepts and in being faced by potential splits in the group and in themselves. They have also enjoyed being in a position to teach the instructor something about behavior therapy.

**Instructor:**   Well, it would be interesting to try some translation. But anyway, it seems that what you were taught before is different from what I am teaching you.

**Carl:** Yes, at least some of the things we were taught, and I think that is troublesome, at least to me with this client.

Carl, with the support of the rest of the seminar, has now identified one aspect of what has been bothering him. It is noteworthy that consensus of the other seminar members frequently encouraged a student to develop and talk about issues that he or she might otherwise have felt reluctant to broach to the instructor.

**Instructor:** Should we be more specific? I think Carl is right; this is one of the things that have been getting in his way.

**Doug:** I think it's tied to the word *contract*. In my head when I hear "contract," the first thing that pops into my head is "behavior." Very structured behavior. You make a contract to modify behavior in a definite way. You make ground rules.

**Instructor:** *Ground rules* and *contract* are not synonymous, but they are related.

**Harriet:** I can't see that you can take at face value what any client says is bothering him. I think you have to work through to what exactly is the problem, so that he can look at himself.

**Instructor:** Your training has been a little different from that of some of the other seminar members, hasn't it?

**Harriet:** Yes, not so behavioral.

**Instructor:** I think that everyone, after his apprenticeship, works out a way for himself. But at the moment you're in a difficult situation. You've been taught one thing; you're not sure you want to go along all the way with it. Now you're being taught another thing, and maybe you don't want to go along with that all the way, either.

**Carl:** It is hard to know what to do now. I had the thought with this girl that she lacked social skills, when she said that she scarcely ever dated. That would be the behavioral formulation and the goal would be to get her to raise the frequency of dating. I thought about the companion service for her, too.

Carl is referring to a service provided by the university through a group of trained undergraduates working in conjunction with a counselor. The undergraduates use behavior change techniques with clients who have skill deficiencies in social situations.

**Instructor:** Interesting, isn't it, that those thoughts were not mentioned before in your presentation?

**Carl:** (laughs) Yes, rather. It just hit home to me that when I get into one set or the other, I just stay in that set for a while. When I'm thinking behaviorally and a client comes in, I say to myself, "Aha, this will be a really good behavioral case." But if I'm thinking more in a relationship set or an insight set, then I see it that way. But it's really hard to know which way one ought to go.

**Instructor:** This is an important problem and may often get in your way. It surely reflects the difficulty in dealing with the new authority figure with whom you are in contact right now.

**Allan:** There's another problem. The behavioral method works sometimes.

**Instructor:** Is that a problem?

**Allan:** Yes.

**Instructor:** Why?

**Allan:** Because I don't feel comfortable. With this girl, for example, I wouldn't feel comfortable doing just behavioral. There is an awful lot of other stuff going on, I feel.

**Doug:** You would do different things, depending on your orientation. If you did a behavior contract, for example, with this client, you would want to increase the frequency of dating behavior, and you would structure it in such a way that if the client does the things she has contracted to do, her dating behavior will increase. If you're working in insight or relationship therapy, you're going at it from the other end. You're hoping to develop something inside her that will make her able to go out and make contacts and develop something herself. But the increased frequency of dating might be a measure of improvement in both cases.

**Instructor:** Just offhand, I'm not willing to buy that as a sure measurement of improvement. Suppose she decides dating is not important to her; she has some other goal. I would not work against her goal unless I were sure it represented a neurotic conflict that would be likely to give her trouble later. The main thing is that she should decide what she wants; the dating is secondary.

**Harriet:** Doesn't it depend on what goals the client wants to set?

**Instructor:** It also depends on whether you can go along with those goals. Some people might feel that they couldn't go along if the client wants to become a more effective revolutionary or a more effective reactionary. Others might feel they couldn't really keep an open mind about a client's wish to enter a convent or a monastery. If a client came to me and said, "I want to get over my inhibitions so that I can become a more effective murderer," I would say, "No, thank you. I'm not in that business. What made you think I was?" But I must say that has never happened to me.

**Carl:** To come back to my case, the question seems to me to be whether I was going along with an unreasonable and unrealistic goal in not challenging her formulation that she wanted to decide about having children when she is only eighteen and there are no external pressures on her to make such a decision.

**Ellen:** That formulation of hers must be covering up something else and that is what brought us to the dating behavior. If she is afraid of dating, she might well rationalize and say, "I never want to have children anyway, so why bother with a relationship with a guy?"

**Gail:** If you let her think you are willing to work on that decision, you also let her think that she has pulled the wool over your eyes, so I think it would be very important to say that you would like to understand why that seems like an urgent question to her when it is actually not urgent at all.

**Carl:**   I guess you are right. It is a formulation that covers up, and I could have moved faster and more clearly with her if I had said something like what you just suggested. I don't really think it would be very hard to get her to see that, and to say that she would like to be able to date more.

**Bob:**   Well, if she sees that and wants that, then you have to decide how to work with her on it, whether behaviorally or with insight therapy.

**Carl:**   I don't know what would be best for me, which set would work best for me.

**Instructor:**   When you say "what would be best for *me*," I'd like to know who is the client around here.

**Carl:**   (Laughing.) Me, of course. I thought that was understood when we joined the seminar. We're all clients.

The general laughter following Carl's reply indicates not only a good feeling of fellowship but also some uneasiness about the self-revelation to which the students have agreed but about which they naturally continue to feel anxious.

**Carl:**   That brings it back to the contract then, doesn't it—and to why I didn't question her formulation of the problem?

**Instructor:**   Yes, I think that is the important point and it takes precedence over what technique you are going to use in treating her. I think we got into these questions about behavioral versus psychodynamic therapy by asking what made you go along with that formulation. And it seemed to emerge in the discussion that you were hung up on the question of which teacher to follow. You are already making a psychodynamic interpretation in assuming that this girl wants to date more. And you are inclined to use behavioral techniques, like the companion service, for example, to accomplish this goal. So I hear your ambivalence about your teachers and their theories.

**Gail:**   The trouble is that I can't separate how I think about the theories from how I feel about the people who stand for them.

**Ellen:** Don't you think there's a connection? I mean some kinds of people go with some kinds of theories?

**Bob:** You'd have a hard time to say what the characteristics are, though.

**Gail:** Well, some put your back up and some don't.

**Allan:** That's an operational definition, all right, but I don't think it distinguishes between behaviorists and psychoanalysts.

**Carl:** I notice it's easier to follow whichever teacher we have right now.

**Instructor:** You might notice that your clients have the same tendency. You are the person in authority right now for them. While they're with you, they tend to follow your teaching and your way of thinking. The brave ones may do otherwise; also the compulsively rebellious ones.

**Carl:** Are you saying if we were brave we'd do behavior therapy and report it in here?

**Instructor:** Why not?

**Ellen:** There's a good reason why not. We want to learn something else from you. We want to learn about psychodynamic psychotherapy. That's why we signed up for this course. I really want to learn what you have to teach.

**Carl:** Ellen is right, of course, but it's not just a matter of behavior therapy. It takes courage to do *anything* your instructor doesn't approve of—yet I often want to do just that.

Ellen represents the conforming aspect of the seminar here. She gives a rational, mature reason for the kind of therapy she proposes to do. Carl speaks for the oppositional side. There are rational and irrational elements in both which appear many times in the seminar. These are dealt with more fully in Chapter Twelve on The Antitherapeutic Aspects of the Seminar. The tension between the wish to please and the wish to oppose the instructor is a constant accompaniment of the case presentations. It is commented on only when it grossly interferes with the work, since the major task of this group is not to study its own behavior but to facilitate the work with clients.

**Gail:** One saving grace is that you can't always be sure what Dr. R. is going to approve and disapprove of, so you have to fall back on yourself. That makes it both harder and easier.

**Allan:** But I do think, if you have the contract clear in your own mind, you usually save time and you don't let things slip by. At least that's the way it is with me. I think this girl not only wants to date more; she also wants to understand what is going on with her. This crazy formulation about having or not having children was the best she could do just now. She's really asking you to help her see what she's up to. When she sees that, you can send her to the companion service to help her improve her social skills if you want to and if she wants to.

**Carl:** It is a lot clearer now and I think I can work with her better.

Carl has confirmed an underlying assumption of the seminar, namely, that clarification of the question facilitates therapeutic work. Having come out with his hidden wish to do just exactly whatever it is that the instructor will not approve of, he is able to make a more rational and mature choice about what form of therapy he will use with this particular client. As long as the issue of following or rebelling against authority was kept out of awareness, the therapeutic process was muddled and would have remained muddled, whether behavioral or psychodynamic methods were being used. Carl, like Ellen and the others, is in the seminar because on a rational level he wants to learn what this particular instructor has to teach. But that does not keep his rebelliousness from being a dynamic force in his actions. The discussion helped him to free himself from his entanglement in compulsive opposition, about which he had not been clear.

The other seminar members shared his conflict, which went much deeper than an intellectual argument between psychodynamic and behavioral theory. Attitudes toward authority play a central role in group life, sometimes furthering, sometimes hindering the tasks which groups and organizations have to perform. As the seminar members became more aware of their attitudes, both rational and irrational, toward the authority of the instructor, they were able to be more open in their doubts and conflicts about theories and techniques.

In this particular case, Carl decided to try to interpret his client's doubts about her ability to be a loving and attractive woman. As she faced these doubts, her behavior in social situations changed. She became more self-confident, and the question with which she had originally approached the therapist disappeared.

For the instructor, the problem in listening to students' reports of their work lay in distinguishing between unconventional interventions that sprang from productive originality in approaching the interpersonal situation and unconventional interventions that sprang from negativism toward her authority. Every teacher faces similar problems. The best solution is often to let this distinction be made by the students themselves as they reflect upon their work.

# CHAPTER 4

# NEGATIVE FEELINGS TOWARD CLIENTS

In this chapter students are struggling with a very common problem that besets beginning therapists and also more experienced ones. The client arouses in them dislike, frustration, or some primarily negative attitude. Since therapists supposedly don't hate their clients, these attitudes are pushed out of awareness, with varying degrees of success. In the four sections that follow, seminar members further the course of therapy by bringing the negative attitudes to the attention of the presenting student and by helping to make these attitudes understandable. The therapist is enabled to get out of the knot in which he felt himself to be inextricably tied.

## Section 1
## The Client Who Cannot Make a Decision

When a client comes for therapy, the presenting problem is often a difficult decision that he feels he has to make. "Should I get a divorce?" "Should I leave my job?" "Should we have another child?" Therapists are usually trained not to give answers to such questions. The clarification that comes through presenting the questions to another person often helps the client to make his own decision. But sometimes, as in the following case, the question persists ad nauseam. Karen, a young woman who is employed as a medical technician and is living with her boyfriend, asks: "Should I stay with this man or break off with him?" The pros and cons have all been stated a million times and nothing has changed. The sessions sound like a broken record. The task of the seminar in this case lay in helping the therapist, Bob, become aware of how tired and resentful he was of the client and in helping him to take a fresh view of the problem.

**Bob:**    I have had seven sessions, once a week, with her, and I feel I need to go through each one of them. I want to get an idea of what's going on. I feel there are recurring themes, but I'm not focusing in on them.

Bob goes on to relate at length what had been happening in four of the sessions in much detail, including discussions of relations with Karen's parents, employer, women friends, and especially with Bill, the man with whom she is living. As she skips about among the various topics, she returns again and again to the question of whether she should leave him or marry him.

**Bob:**    This last session was around her birthday, and she was hoping her boyfriend would give her a present, but he didn't. She was very hurt, so she pouted the whole next day, and when he asked her what was the trouble, she said, "Oh, it really doesn't matter." But she didn't speak to him for two days. I pointed out that she doesn't say what is on her mind. She keeps making the boyfriend look like the worst guy around, like somebody that any girl would have to be crazy to maintain a relationship with. After she has presented that image, she turns around and says he really does a lot of good things, too. Then she goes on to present the negative again. Just when she gets to the point you would think she'd be realizing this is a totally bad relationship, she starts going in the other direction. She'll say, "I can't really imagine us breaking up, but then there is always a possibility." The relationship puts her under a lot of strain, but then she says, "I am the only one he has to count on," and he tells her she is his only true friend. When she is thinking she will stay with him and marry him, she begins to worry about his leaving her. She was also talking about her woman friend who is getting married and is very happy.

Bob continues poring through his notes for some time, giving examples of Karen's jumping from topic to topic but returning continually to the question, To leave or to marry the boyfriend? The variation on the question is, To be left or to leave first?

**Doug:**   I wonder if you would stop looking through your notes and going back over everything. Why don't you just say what is bothering you about this girl?

The seminar members have been unusually tolerant up to this point in listening without interrupting to a presentation which was, by and large, remarkably unenlightening about the client. Probably they felt correctly Bob's struggle with himself and his conscientious effort to do a good job. Doug is the first one to break into the rather droning recital and to express some of the impatience that other seminar members were also feeling.

**Bob:**   You think that might be more beneficial to me?

**Doug:**   I'm getting the feeling that—well, I'm just getting very uncomfortable. I'm not sure what is going on, but it is as if you feel you have to go into all these details and I don't know what you're getting at.

**Bob:**   Is it boring?

**Doug:**   Well, I'm at a loss—.

Doug hesitates to hurt Bob's feelings. The truth is that he and others have been bored for some time. He might more usefully have stated his feelings at this point.

**Bob:** Maybe I'm doing the same thing that she does. She presents so much and nothing happens. Maybe I'm doing the same thing. Is that what you're saying?

**Doug:** I guess it is.

**Bob:** All right. I'll leave my notes, and just say what I remember. In the next to the last session, no, in the next to the next to the last session, she said, "This is really going to be heavy. I think I broke up with Bill." When she went home to her parents' house for the weekend he didn't even kiss her goodbye. He just said "see ya" or something like that. And when she came back they started to fight, and Bill told her she was acting like a baby and she walked out. She didn't seem very upset. She just talked about being afraid he would never marry her anyway, and she kept asking me if she should go back to him.

**Gail:** You mean, whether she should change her mind again and go back to him?

**Bob:** Right. I had the feeling the whole time that she would go back. And the next session she came in and said they were back together again. She said it had been a great week! She hadn't been finding so many things wrong with Bill. She also said she had gone back because I had implied she should. She has been asking me constantly since the beginning what I think she should do, and I never gave her any opinion. This time I decided I would call her bluff and give her my opinion and see what she would do. She had just asked me: "You really think I should live with Bill, don't you?" And I said, "Yes, I think you should." I really just wanted to see what would happen. I wasn't planning to leave it that way without explaining. I wanted to see what her reaction would be. She was really surprised and said, "Why did you say that? Why did you give me your opinion?" I said, "You've been asking me all along, and I felt you really wanted to know what I was thinking."

**Instructor:** That was not entirely true, was it?

**Bob:** No, it wasn't. She said, "You think Bill isn't right for me, and you want me to find out for myself." Then she started complaining that it was Bill and I against her. I pointed out that that was her idea, not mine, and she agreed. Then she went on with all the reasons why she couldn't live with Bill and why it was good that I don't give her advice.

**Instructor:** Right after you had given her advice?

**Bob:** Yes, right. Well, I pointed out that when I finally gave her advice, she realized she couldn't use it. I told her the reason I had said, "Yes, you should live with Bill," was because I wanted to see what her reaction would be. She wanted to know whether I knew in advance what her reaction would be, that she would say, "Well, you don't know all the facts, so you really can't give an opinion." I told her I really didn't know what she would do, but I wanted her to know that I couldn't be of help by offering my opinion. Then she said she didn't really need me to give an opinion anyhow, because she had decided to live with Bill. Then she went on about why she might not want to live with him.

**Instructor:** Right after she said she had made the decision to do it?

**Bob:** Yes, right. I might be making this a little confusing.

**Carl:** Could we hear a little bit of the tape?

The seminar listens for a while to a very boring taped recital of why she should or should not stay or leave. The voice is monotonous, without much affect but with a suggestion of underlying depression.

**Harriet:** Can you stand to hear any more?

**Doug:** No.

**Instructor:** I can't either.

**Ellen:** How can you stand it in the sessions, Bob?

**Bob:**    Well, in the last session I just laid the cards on the table. I said the overwhelming thing she had presented to me was that this wasn't the right guy, but maybe the guy who isn't the right guy is better than no guy at all; maybe it's better to have a bad relationship than none.

**Instructor:**    What did she make of that?

**Bob:**    She thought about it. She started to talk again, but her voice trailed off. She said she knows she should get rid of him, but she can't. But maybe he will leave her.

Bob has now summarized concisely the dilemma his client thinks she is in: whether to put up with a miserable relationship or to have none. The seminar begins to come alive.

**Instructor:**    That's a pretty unhappy situation, isn't it?

**Bob:**    Yes, it is. I repeated it to her and then she said, "I can't look at bad things."

**Carl:**    Are you bored with this girl?

**Bob:**    No.

**Instructor:**    You're not? What interests you about her?

**Allan:**    My feeling is, if you weren't bored, you were sure awfully close to it.

**Bob:**    Well, sometimes I have been bored, but not the last session. What happened was, I taped one session and played it for some of the counselors in the agency and they said that I was just indulging her by letting her go on the way I did.

**Ellen:**    Which is what we did with you today.

**Bob:**    Right, but in the last session I didn't do that. What happened was that she said she thought she was ready to terminate with me. She now knew the problem. I suggested that maybe she felt I was making her choose between me and the boyfriend. I don't think I said it quite as strongly as that, but along those lines. I was very conscious of trying not to do anything that would manipulate her into coming back.

**Gail:** Do you think she should come back?

**Bob:** Yes, I do think so.

**Gail:** Well, then why didn't you tell her so?

**Bob:** I guess I felt like—well, when I discussed it with the other people in the agency, they made me feel like I was meeting my needs rather than hers. In other words, I needed a client. I was thinking, "What will the seminar say; what will Dr. R. say, if I lose my client?" That's what I was really hung up with.

This important point is elaborated in Chapter Twelve. It occurred often that the pressure exerted by the seminar and the instructor kept the students from concentrating on their clients' interest. The students' need to keep their clients in therapy at all costs was uppermost in their minds.

**Instructor:** I must say that we see again the unhappy influence of the seminar and of supervision and also of well-meaning colleagues. But let's leave that for now. Did you think Karen should return for her own sake, quite apart from your own needs?

**Bob:** Yes.

**Instructor:** Well, that's the thing that's important. It's too bad that all those other things came in to keep you from saying it. "Manipulation" is a dirty word, and nobody wants to be accused of that. Suppose we use the word "influence." It seems to me that it is our responsibility as therapists to state our position about whether we think the therapy should continue if we think a client is stopping prematurely. Obviously, the client doesn't have to do what we say, but she may infer from your not saying anything that you agreed with her. It is often very surprising and enlightening to hear from clients months later what they have made of our silences.

**Harriet:** I was struck by the deadening feeling we got from your presentation. And when it got more lively it seemed that Karen wanted to terminate.

**Doug:** Yes, I was impressed by how low your affect was all the way through, especially in the beginning.

**Carl:**   Your voice was hypnotic to the point of being soporific, and that's not the way you usually speak.

**Instructor:**   I do think a number of people, including myself, were bored, and we wondered how you were putting up with it.

**Bob:**   I finally did get a bit impatient. And then I stopped letting her ramble and tried to stick with the one issue and to point out to her every time she went away from it.

**Harriet:**   I wonder if Bill is the problem. That's where the focus has been and you haven't got off dead center. I don't really think he's the problem at all.

**Bob:**   Well, you all told me that last time I presented, but I can't seem to get her to—she just manages to get me away.

**Instructor:**   How does that happen?

**Bob:**   I think what happens is that she bombards me with so much that I'm always busy trying to catch up with what she's saying.

**Ellen:**   I don't see how you stand it.

**Instructor:**   I don't think you should stand it, actually. As long as you listen she will keep on. Eternal tolerance is not always therapeutic.

**Allan:**   I get a fantasy of this old bossy-cow chewing its cud over and over.

**Instructor:**   And yet this girl keeps coming, so that one has to assume that there is a human being behind all this crap and that this human being is suffering. That, I think, is what you're missing. You go along with all this endless "Should I live with him or shouldn't I live with him?", and it is enough to drive anybody up the wall. The difficulty is to cut through all this to get to the suffering human being. You can be sure that there is someone there, but it takes a bit of energy and strong-mindedness to get to it and not to put up with the nonsense. And in the process she may leave. That is something you have to recognize. She may just stop coming, but I don't see that there is much good in her coming with just this kind of stuff going on. I think everybody here felt this was unbearable and wondered how you had stood it this long.

**Allan:** If you could get away from the subject of the decision, which is certainly not the real problem, you would be better off.

**Instructor:** I think Allan is right. As things are, I can't see that it makes any difference if she stays with him or doesn't stay with him. In a way, they were made for each other since they seem to be able to put up with each other quite well. But that doesn't matter. The thing is for you to try to get at what you think is the problem underneath all this and to stay with it.

**Bob:** I guess that's my trouble. I'm not sure what the problem is. I've tried to stay with the decision.

**Allan:** Well, I guess I would question that. I'm not sure that's the crux of it.

**Bob:** What do you mean?

**Allan:** Well, I think she is trying to tell you that she *has* to stay in that relationship. I think part of the reason may be guilt feelings over the sexual involvement. I'm just speculating, but I was trying to put myself in your position. I've had two clients like her in the past, and I know the ideas that get beaten into a girl's head and how guilt could mess her up. Even these days she could have a lot of guilt about having sexual relations before she's married. I'm familiar with the kind of background she comes from.

**Carl:** Then it would be very important to her to get married.

**Bob:** Well, I'm a little confused now. I'm picking one thing to focus on with her and you're picking another thing and somebody else might pick another.

Bob has correctly perceived that different therapists might approach the problem from different angles, but he wants to stay with his own. The seminar members are tending to make up for their long-suffering silence by asserting their own views.

They also sense that Bob is allowing more of his negative feelings to come into his awareness.

**Fran:**   Maybe we're too focused on the content and not on what's going on. I was thinking she is conveying that she doesn't think much of herself and she feels very separate from everybody else, and I'm wondering if you feel that way when you're with her. It seems like you're sitting at opposite corners of the room, and there's not much positive between you.

**Bob:**   Do you mean I feel isolated from her?

**Fran:**   Yes, don't you?

**Bob:**   I don't know. I guess I do.

**Instructor:**   In a way you did already say that. When you "put the cards on the table" for her, you were talking essentially about her isolation. You said it seemed she had the choice between a bad relationship or none, a bad marriage or no marriage. If that's the way she sees it, she must feel pretty isolated. And I think we all get a strong feeling of depression from your presentation of this girl. She is depressed, and you are depressed, and both of you are afraid of your negative feelings toward each other.

It is now possible for the instructor to say very directly what has been in the minds of most of the seminar members since the beginning of the session.

**Bob:**   I guess maybe my depression comes from my feeling that Karen actually is stuck in a dilemma.

**Instructor:**   So it seems there's no way out. If that is the situation, if this is the best she can do, then the despair is very understandable.

**Bob:**   I hope she could do better than this, but I don't know how to tell her that. I guess my depression comes from feeling that she might think it's hopeless.

**Instructor:**   I'm not sure that you do see any way out for her, and I think that's why you're depressed. Even though you say you don't see it the way you think she does, I'm not sure you really believe that, because your sense of depression comes across so strongly in the presentation. You seem to feel hopeless, too.

**Bob:** I feel kind of trapped, in that I would like to tell her what to do and I feel I can't tell her what to do.

**Instructor:** You seem to be caught in a dilemma, too. I think you bought her way of seeing the situation, which you formulated very well: "All you have is a choice between this bad relationship and no relationship."

**Bob:** You mean you feel that I believe that? You think I have such a low opinion of her?

**Instructor:** Yes.

**Bob:** I think there ought to be other possibilities for her, but I guess I do feel that she is going to stay in this relationship because it seems like such a terrible thing to her to break off. She has to keep this boyfriend.

**Instructor:** Well, I think that indicates that you don't see any way out, and that is the reason for your depression. You are assuming that she will remain the way she is, but that it would be a good thing for her to leave this unsatisfactory relationship. But so long as she remains the way she is, she cannot leave the relationship. She is terribly isolated, as Harriet pointed out, but living with the boyfriend obscures that and takes the edge off it, though he makes her pay a high price for the alleviation of her sense of isolation. Could you and she take a new view of the situation and ask what it is that makes her so isolated in or out of the relationship with that particular man?

**Doug:** She has a totally awful concept of herself as unimportant.

**Bob:** We have gotten into it sometimes about how unimportant she is.

**Instructor:** I'm a little bit unhappy myself about the formulation of "I'm not important," because who is important? Importance depends on how much society needs one or wants one. Either everybody is important or you have to grade people according to how much they're needed or wanted in society, and some people are more in demand than others. I would wonder if perhaps a formulation in terms of low self-esteem might be more workable. It may come to the same thing, but the question is how to formulate it in a way that makes sense to you and to her and is workable. Since she had told you the real reason she stays with this fellow is that she's afraid she's not worthy of anyone else, that really clinches it, doesn't it?

**Bob:**   I guess it does.

**Instructor:**   Here's a young woman who thinks she can never find any partner except this one single person whom she doesn't like. She must feel there's something deeply wrong with her.

**Bob:**   I was just thinking. She has sometimes said she has a low self-image, and I don't think I was picking up on it. I was blind to it because I didn't know what to do with it or why she has it.

**Allan:**   And because you don't like her.

**Bob:**   You really think I don't?

**Instructor:**   Well, why should you? I think the painful thing for her to come face to face with is that she is doing something herself every day to sustain this low self-image. She's racing off in all directions to keep from seeing this. You've tried a little bit to show it to her, but you've got to hold her firmly to it, and at the same time kindly, and it's not easy, because she will try to get away.

**Bob:**   Well, I can't stand going on the way we have been.

**Instructor:**   I'm glad to hear you say that. As we listened to the tape, I think all of us were experiencing something near despair. I don't know whether you experienced that.

**Allan:**   You certainly sounded depressed.

**Bob:**   I guess I am, because I'm saying to myself, "How could I have been so blind, doing the same thing over and over again?"

**Instructor:** Well, could you take that question seriously? I think it might throw some light on Karen and your relationship with her. You are asking yourself, "How could I be so blind?"

**Bob:** Yes, how could I not see the forest for the trees? I've just been going through the same thing over and over.

**Instructor:** Yes, I think you have. Now you ask yourself, "How could that be?"

**Bob:** I guess I'm just expressing the disappointment and, as Allan says, dislike.

**Instructor:** Yes, I understand, Bob, but if you could now turn that into a truly investigative question instead of just throwing blame at yourself, I think you might learn something about the relationship that would allow you to work with her in a different way. How did it happen that you both got on this merry-go-round?

**Bob:** Because she couldn't bring herself to talk about her actual feelings. She has to get away a little bit and go where it's safe.

**Ellen:** A little bit?

**Bob:** Well, a lot.

**Ellen:** Bob, might it be that you were overconcerned to have a good relationship with her, I mean to have her feel comfortable in order to be able to work with her? If you insisted on talking about disagreeable things, she might leave.

**Harriet:** Or Karen may end up not liking Bob.

**Allan:** Up to now she's been speaking in a very complimentary way about you.

**Instructor:** Yes, she may have some not-so-pleasant thoughts about you but you don't really have a choice any more. I think one measure of the degree of desperation you were pushed to was this experiment that you tried of telling her she should live with Bill, or she shouldn't live with him. I don't remember which you told her and it doesn't matter. It seems to me when you're pushed to that kind of thing with a client it's very dangerous for the relationship, for how will she ever know from now on when you're "experimenting" and when you're talking straight? A student told me once about an experiment that was done when she was an undergraduate in a sociology class. It was done without telling the class it was an experiment. She never trusted anything that was said by the professor from then on. And she is not a paranoid person either. One might think it would be even more serious in a therapeutic situation for the client not to know when you are playing manipulative tricks. It adds to the general distrust of authority that we have seen all too much of in our public life. You are taking an extremely distant position from the client, running her like a rat in a maze. Fortunately, Karen doesn't seem to hear much of what you say, so perhaps it didn't make much of an impression on her any more than the good things you have said. I think it is a measure of the despair you were feeling that you got into this.

**Bob:** Well, I think it won't be so bad now if it turns out she doesn't like me and even if she leaves.

**Doug:** I think it's very hard to be with anybody who is depressed, and if you can sort of keep saying to yourself, "I'm getting depressed and this feeling is contagious," that somehow helps you not to get the depression into the way you think. You can get detached from that feeling of depression.

**Instructor:** That's a very important point, but first you have to be aware of how depressed you actually are. I think we were all aware of it in your presentation, but I'm not sure that you were sufficiently aware of your depression and the resentment underlying it.

**Bob:** I think one of my biggest problems was that I really was very concerned about the presentation. I guess what I wanted to do was to give you as much as possible. Actually I think you were all falling asleep.

**Ellen:** I wonder if that is what she is doing to you and that is one of the ways she drives people away.

Bob:    I think that's true. You have gotten through to me on that.

This session illustrates that the seminar can be helpful, even in a difficult and depressing situation, when the members are supportive and at the same time honest with the presenting student. It is difficult to know what makes this possible. The mood of the seminar is dependent on many factors, not always definable. In this case the genuineness of Bob's wish for help and his quite appealing honesty seem to have warded off the sharp criticism that greeted some of the other presentations.

Karen had bombarded Bob over and over again with the same question in various forms. Neither he nor she could seem to think of anything else. She was depressed and near despair at not being able to make and stay with a decision. Bob was valiantly trying to conceal from himself his boredom and resentment at having to hear her monotonous repetition without any resolution. Before any therapeutic movement could take place, Bob had to become aware of how tired he was of Karen's endless recitals of the same thing. In this the seminar members were eminently helpful in giving Bob "permission" to experience his angry weariness and resentment. Once that was done, it was possible for him to see that the question "Should I leave or should I stay?" was a smoke screen that the client used to keep herself from thinking the unthinkable, namely that she is an impossible human being. Bob has come dangerously close to believing the same thing by tolerating her superficial complaints to the point of simply wanting to get rid of her. Only when he becomes aware of the extent of his resentment can he ask and answer the question that is at the bottom of all this. What makes this young woman drive herself and others to despair? When he can do this, it becomes possible for him to present Karen with a new view of her situation. Her "impossibility" as a human being is not a genetic given, but a modifiable pattern of behavior.

The client who repeats the same thing over and over again, whether in words or in deeds, is almost certain to arouse negative feelings in the therapist; he then becomes not only bored but impotent to do anything to stop the eternal complaints. In this case Bob was caught in the vicious circle that Karen had set up for herself. The endless repetition of her complaints made her feel unworthy. And because she felt unworthy, she complained endlessly. Her complaints drove people away, and, because people were driven away, she complained. When a therapist becomes clear about a vicious circle of this kind, he can comment on it with determination not to be sucked into the despair that it engenders and that engenders it. His ability to comment on the vicious circle means that he has stepped outside it, at least for a moment. Then he can try to persuade his client to also step out of it and to view it from a distance. As soon as the therapist is persuaded that his client *can* do something better, he can help him to realize that he who set the circle in motion can also stop it.

## Section 2
## The Client Who Claims Nothing Is Wrong

The therapist's negative feelings for her client in this section have built up quite understandably on the basis of the latter's bland denial that anything is wrong, when there is abundant evidence that almost everything is wrong. The therapist had swallowed so much anger that she feared it might explode. The only alternative seemed to be withdrawal. The difficulty, as well as the solution, to the problem seemed to lie in ferreting out something to work on.

The client in this excerpt is a young man who complained initially of feeling confused. He was separated from his wife, in process of getting a divorce, and was dating another woman with whom he had a tenuous and increasingly troubled relationship. The client was thinking vaguely that there might be something that led to his forming unfortunate relationships, but in the five sessions he had had with the therapist he had made no progress in discovering what that might be. Harriet is presenting.

**Harriet:** When I asked him to tell me about his family, he just said, "There's nothing wrong with my family. Everyone got along very well. No one has any problems." When I asked him about his marriage, he said he had noted some disagreements during the engagement and had wondered at the time if he was making a mistake, but somehow it seemed inevitable that they should get married, so he did it. More difficulties emerged after they got married, so he decided he wanted to separate. He told his wife and she did not object. For the life of me I cannot get a clear picture of these "difficulties" that they had. At the time he said he wanted a divorce, he was already dating another woman. She was married, having trouble with her husband, and they commiserated with each other. Then she went back to her husband and that ended. Now there is still another woman, and they are having some disagreements already. When I try to ask for specifics, he becomes terribly nervous, shifts around in his chair, smokes, changes the subject, and becomes vague. I point this out to him, and he seems not to hear. After the fourth time I did it in one session, he said, "Am I really so tense? Do you really think I am a nervous wreck?" I said I was observing his behavior and asking what he made of it himself. He finds one or another way to evade questions of that kind. One time he said he didn't want to talk about that; he wanted to find out what made him confused and whether he always would choose the wrong women.

**Allan:** Does he say that he's dissatisfied with anything in himself besides his confusion?

**Harriet:** It's very hard for him to talk about things like that. I had the idea that maybe he thought he was a dangerous person and if people got too close to him he would do something awful to them.

**Instructor:** Did you present that possibility to him?

**Harriet:** Yes, and, well, he kind of agreed, and then that was the end of it. I also thought that in his relationships he is torn between a desire for great intimacy and a fear of it. I said that, and he kind of agreed to that, too, but I didn't get the sense that it had any meaning for him.

**Instructor:**   Do you think he's reacting to you the same way he does to his family, saying there's nothing wrong and everyone is getting along well?

**Harriet:**   Yes, I do think so, and I don't know how to break through it. I wish I knew how to help him.

Harriet's voice betrays considerable irritation. Her facial expression, usually pleasant and friendly, has become something between a scowl and a sulk.

**Instructor:**   It's possible that you have other wishes, too.

**Harriet:**   I don't understand.

This intervention on the part of the instructor came too soon and without preparation. Harriet is not yet ready to come out with the full force of the frustration and anger that she feels toward this client.

**Ellen:**   I think I'd be wishing for some magic.

**Gail:**   When we listened to a part of your tape you sounded very patient and accepting, but a little bored, too. Now, when you talk about him to us, you sound annoyed.

**Harriet:**   I guess the boredom is covering my annoyance. He just doesn't seem to have any idea what other people are like, except in the most external terms. When I asked him about his wife, he said she was attractive and she dressed well.

**Gail:**   That's interesting. The impression I was getting of him while you were talking was of an outline drawing.

**Harriet:**   Yes, that's the way he seems to me.

**Bob:**   That's a very safe posture.

**Instructor:**   But he doesn't feel good about it, or he wouldn't be coming to see you.

**Harriet:**   I'm afraid that if I insist on his noticing his discomfort and working on it, I'll be too unkind to him.

Harriet has now formulated her problem clearly. Her

anger at her client has built up to such an extent that it actually frightens her. She is so preoccupied with keeping herself under control during the sessions that she is paralyzed and does not function effectively.

**Instructor:** I think that you and he have a choice to make: Will you or won't you go through a period of anxiety and upheaval that will enable an inner change to take place? Your fear that you may be unkind to him is what is standing in your way. He's not likely to move until *you* do. You *could* leave him in his rut. As Bob was saying, it seems like a safe posture. If you don't leave him there, you have to go through some discomfort with him. That's your responsibility. It's not a unilateral decision, of course. He can go along with you or not, but you do have to decide.

**Harriet:** Well, if I don't, there's probably no point in continuing with him. Nothing is happening.

**Allan:** This is a case where I think responsibility should be spelled *response-ability*. It's your client's and your ability to respond to another person, really.

**Instructor:** Yes, and I'd like to raise the question as to whether any significant change is likely to take place in a person without some discomfort. This holds for us in this seminar as well as for our clients. I'm taking issue with the idea that learning is or should always be pleasant and positive. I question that. Isn't it necessary to go through a certain amount of discomfort if learning is to take place? I mean that both for us and the client.

**Ellen:** My feeling is stronger than that. I think when a person comes to you he expects to be stirred up. They don't expect you to let them continue in a comfortable way. If you do, the client could see you as someone they have put something over on, and your effectiveness is destroyed.

**Doug:** I thought you were asking how much is too much for this client, Harriet.

**Harriet:** I was, but I think the thing that I really am afraid of is not that I will make him so uncomfortable but that I will make myself so uncomfortable I won't know what I'm doing.

**Instructor:**    In the meantime, he's frustrating the hell out of you and that may be the basis of your fear. So far he's a very unrewarding client. You started out with a promise from the intake interviewer that he would be a "motivated" patient, and look what he's doing. Nothing. You wonder what you're spending your time for. It must be rising up in you to really put a little bomb under him. Is that a temptation?

**Harriet:**    My temptation is simply to forget the whole thing, to withdraw and let him withdraw and discontinue therapy.

**Instructor:**    But then if you don't allow yourself to withdraw, if you say to yourself, "That's not what a good therapist does," then the opposite of that is to move in too hard, isn't it? And this is what you're afraid of.

**Harriet:**    Yes, I think that's true. I guess I would enjoy planting a bomb under his chair.

**Instructor:**    There are two possibilities, and there are two dangers: one to withdraw and the other to move in too hard. The third alternative is the therapeutic way out, namely to notice and observe the two extremes, the dangers you might become involved in. You can see the immense amount of pressure he's putting on you to do one or the other of these two things. I think you always have to remember that you may not be able to do anything about it. It's his decision, ultimately, but you could present it to him more firmly and consistently.

Having recognized her anger at the client, Harriet was able to take a stronger stand without the danger that she had envisioned of being too "unkind." This client was among those whom therapists speak of as being not "psychologically minded." He did not observe his own feelings and behavior or the subtle responses of others toward him. Harriet had a long, arduous task ahead to teach him to become more observant both of himself and others. She had to use herself as an example of how he irritated others without recognizing that he was doing so or why he was doing it. He had learned early in life that in his family it was better to deny any feelings than to admit them into consciousness. Clients like this do not strip off their character armor in one glorious moment in response to a therapist's decision to move into the discomfort of negative feelings. Harriet had to struggle often with the problem of her irritation and her wish to withdraw from it and from him. The rewards were slow in coming, but Harriet learned not to let her anger build to the point where she feared she might become destructive.

## Section 3
## The Client Who Resembles the Therapist

The client who resembles the therapist in some important ways is apt to present special problems. The therapist may find himself smiling indulgently and inappropriately at some precious aspect of himself that he finds charming. But sometimes, as in this case, the crucial resemblance has to do with a behavior pattern of which the therapist strongly disapproves. The fact that this is out of awareness does not improve matters. The work of this session consisted in helping Fran, who is the presenting student, to become aware of the troublesome aspect of her resemblance to her client.

Fran is presenting a thirty-year-old woman who has recently separated from her husband. She has no children, and she claims she would like to marry again, but all her relationships with men have gone on the rocks. Fran has given in great detail her client's quite disturbed early history and the course of her therapy with the client over the past several months. Just before she stops her presentation she makes the following statement.

**Fran:**    I thought at first this client would be especially easy for me. I know her background well, because it is a lot like mine. I thought she even looked something like me, so it ought to be easy for me to understand her, and it was, at first. But now she doesn't get any better, and she just seems stuck in her old patterns. I wish you could help me see what is the trouble.

**Doug:**   (Quite sharply.) You say that as if you didn't think we could.

**Fran:**   (Equally sharply.) Well, can you?

**Gail:**   I did think you took so long over the history that you didn't leave much time to tell what is now going on in the therapy, and you didn't leave us much time for discussion either.

**Fran:**   (Very defensively.) The history is important.

**Instructor:**   It seems to me you are all in a fighting mood, which is certainly worth noticing. Don't you think it reflects something about the presentation?

**Fran:**   It's true she sometimes makes me feel like a prosecuting attorney. I told her that once, and she agreed; she feels sometimes as if I am prosecuting her, not helping her. I guess in trying to figure out what she does to the men in her life I make her feel guilty. I would really like to understand her better.

**Harriet:**   I thought you were talking awfully fast today. It was not only that you went into a lot of detail in the history but you talked so fast, as if you were very anxious and did not want to look at something and did not want us to interrupt you.

**Allan:**   You said you and she were a lot alike. I should think that would help you to see what she does.

**Fran:**   Well, if I don't see it, I don't see it. I just don't like what she is doing, and it is really very disappointing. Everything is going bad after she made such good progress for a while. I just don't understand it.

Fran is still reacting defensively to the continued attacks by the seminar members. It is clear that not much progress is going to be made so long as the attacks continue. The seminar members are responding to something in Fran's presentation that they have not yet defined. Harriet has pointed out the anxiety evident in the presentation, but the reasons for it are still unclear.

**Ellen:**   I think it is important, Fran, that you didn't tell us you felt so much like the client until the very end of your presentation. Could it be that you are alike not only in externals of looks and background but also in more internal ways that you don't want to think about? If you don't like something in yourself, you might "prosecute" it in her.

**Fran:** (Somewhat hesitatingly.) What do you mean?

Ellen now feels put on the spot and does not want to be entirely frank with Fran. Her answer is, therefore, evasive.

**Ellen:** Well, you might know better than I do. I just mean that happens sometimes. I know I have found myself condemning clients when they do some things that I particularly don't like in myself.

**Fran:** It is kind of scary to think I might be looking into a mirror.

**Carl:** I think what she does with these guys is, she leads them on and is terribly nice to them. When she's got them hooked, she pulls the rug out from under them. She's done it time and again. And now she is doing it to you, too. She let you think you were great and she was making fine progress. And now you're not doing anything for her; you can't understand her and she is getting no better.

Carl's observation is very important and very correct. At the same time, however, it lets Fran off the hook. He is talking about what the client is doing to her, and in the next statement Fran gratefully goes along.

**Fran:** I certainly did feel let down by her. It was all going so well earlier on. Now she isn't budging an inch.

**Instructor:** If you could see what there is in this that makes you uneasy, it would help. Of course, nobody likes it when his clients don't make progress. Carl seems to me to have hit the nail on the head with his description of her pattern. I don't want to go into your personal life. But I would think you would have to ask yourself whether in some subtle ways you may do that, too. That would make it hard for you to keep your therapeutic stance and, as Ellen says, you would try to "prosecute" her for things that you feel guilty about yourself. Do you think that might be making you anxious?

**Fran:**   I feel very tense now in the sessions with her, but sometimes I feel invigorated, too.

**Doug:**   Like you're winning in combat?

**Fran:**   Yes, it's like I'm on the side of the right. It's scary to think that the "wrong" may be in me as well as in her.

**Instructor:**   It may help to remember that the client is presenting you not with a true mirror but with one of those you see in carnivals where you recognize yourself but you are all distorted. You have to remember you are *not* identical with the client, even though she reminds you of yourself in ways that make you uneasy.

**Fran:**   It is still scary, but it helps to think that I am not *just* like her. I do think Ellen was right, too; that's why I was prosecuting her.

**Bob:**   If you were more tolerant of yourself, you would be more tolerant of her, and you could help her to understand herself better.

**Instructor:**   And if you find all that much tolerance too wishy-washy, you can think of it as taking an investigative attitude both toward yourself and your client; that is, you are being a scientist rather than a prosecutor or a judge.

**Fran:**   I guess I really have been furious at this woman for the way she has treated a number of different men, and I guess even more so for treating me the same way. I think I can get a little distance from it now that it has been said. I also recognize some tendencies of my own.

This time the seminar was quite successful in pointing out to the presenting therapist the negative attitude she had toward her client as well as its source. Although Fran was defensive at first, she was honest enough to see quite readily what she was doing. In fact, she made it easy for the seminar members to help her become aware of the basis for her "prosecution" of the client. This case became a paradigm for the seminar in learning to recognize the tendency to project outside oneself disliked qualities or impulses that are active inside oneself. This was an important piece of learning that helped in understanding the mechanism of projection and in understanding a frequent source of therapists' dislike for certain clients.

# CHAPTER 5

# DIFFICULTIES PRESENTED BY A BORDERLINE SCHIZOPHRENIC

This chapter illustrates the difficulties encountered in the treatment of clients who are more disturbed than the usual population of college students.

The inexperienced student of psychotherapy has to start somewhere to see clients. Just as the new surgeon, having mastered the details of anatomy, having observed his professors, and having performed operations on animals, finally has to operate on his first patient, so the psychotherapist has to have his first real client. He may have practiced role-playing, observed through one-way mirrors, or been a cotherapist in a group. But he finally has a client on his own. Whether this is a child in a school for disturbed children, a college student in a counseling center, or a psychotic patient in a hospital usually depends much more on the convenience of the training institution than on a considered plan of what is the best way for a student to begin.

The students in this seminar had had most of their first experiences with college and high school students or outpatients in community agencies. None of them had had any hospital experience. Most of their clients were suffering from relatively mild disorders. Schizophrenic or borderline patients were rare. Thus, when Gail presented a borderline schizophrenic client, it was a new experience for most members of the seminar. This provided a particularly good opportunity to notice a phenomenon that we called "mirroring." By this we meant that the whole group exhibited signs of being in the same frame of mind that the client had seemed to be in during the therapy sessions. The interaction with the presenter "mirrored" the interaction between client and therapist. The students learned to look for this phenomenon and to use their own responses in the seminar as possible indications of what was occurring in the client-therapist interaction. Another example of this phenomenon occurs in Chapter Nine.

Gail is presenting the case of Joan, a seventeen-year-old borderline schizophrenic girl, a student in a small college, whom she has seen three times at intervals of one week. Joan has told some rather fantastic tales about her childhood and described a very disturbed present life. Everyone agrees that once- or twice-a-week therapy on an out-patient basis is not optimal for this young woman; however, unless she were to be institutionalized in a state hospital, there is no practical alternative at this time. Gail states two major concerns: 1) Is she being manipulated by the client in listening to a series of wild tales? 2) Is she doing the best thing for the client by seeing her, or ought she to turn her over to someone else? This second question persists in an irrational way even after alternatives have been discarded.

A question had been raised about alerting Joan's guardians, an uncle and aunt who live halfway across the country. Because the client made a clear statement that she would simply disappear from the city if this were done, the issue was set aside, at least temporarily.

**Gail:** I guess my question—it's not well formulated—is whether she's manipulating me, telling me all these stories. I'm kind of in a spot here. And I feel pulled apart because I don't know what to follow up.

**Bob:** Does she screw around a lot?

**Gail:** No, she's got just one friend, a strange fellow who is a dropout from high school.

**Bob:** Doesn't she date others?

**Gail:** Not much.

**Harriet:** Do you feel that she is manipulating you?

**Gail:** Sure, but what I want to know is—

**Carl:** (Interrupting.) Do you think she's consciously lying?

**Gail:** Maybe sometimes, and I want to know which part I'm taken in by.

**Doug:** I'm not really convinced the uncle and aunt should be brought in.

**Gail:** That's the way I'm feeling right now.

**Fran:** Maybe it's a good thing they live a long way off.

**Ellen:** I was interested in the fact that she came in saying, "I'm crazy."

**Allan:** And then bringing in her short stories that she's written.

**Carl:** Does she have difficulty making decisions? I have a hypothesis about that.

The discussion jumps from one point to another, with each person picking up a different aspect of the case. This is not the usual thing in this group, the members of which are quite capable of staying with one theme until it has been exhausted. It is very much like the dialogue that Gail described between herself and Joan, in which one *non sequitur* occurred after another. A coherent story was hard to piece together.

**Instructor:** It seems to me that you can't be at all sure that what she's telling you is true in any ordinary sense. It is awkward not to know whether you're dealing with fact or fiction. It's also dangerous to try to pin somebody like this down and show her the inconsistencies, because all she'll do is find ways to get out. I think a way around this is to look at everything she's telling you as if she were recounting a dream. Take it with the same seriousness that you would take a dream, as a production of her mind. It's telling you something, but not necessarily the literal truth. Then you have a way out of the dilemma of on the one hand doubting everything she says, with the attitude of "Come on now, prove it," and on the other hand swallowing it all as fact.

**Ellen:** That's the way you take the stories she has written.

**Gail:** Yes, that's so.

**Instructor:** Another thing you can do for her is simply to represent to her something in the world that's solid and steady and dependable. It's probably more important to look at what is really going on in her present life, insofar as you can find it out, than to look at her fantastic stories, both those she's written and those she tells you.

**Gail:** We've done something in that area. She has this relationship with her boyfriend that is destructive for both of them.

**Harriet:** How can you be sure it's destructive, Gail?

**Gail:** Well, they frighten each other and make inordinate demands on each other, and they say terrible things to and about each other.

**Bob:**   Maybe you really should get in touch with her uncle and aunt.

**Instructor:**   Maybe, and it's all true what you are saying, Gail, but I think Harriet has a point. We are quick to say a relationship is destructive, but where would she be without it? At least it is a relationship to another human being and for this girl that isn't so easy to come by. Certainly you want to help her understand what role it plays in her life.

**Allan:**   Gail, have you raised the question of seeing her twice a week?

**Gail:**   Not with her.

The seminar is still jumping from one topic to another. Each isolated comment makes sense but there is no continuity or coherence in the talk. Each comment pulls the presenter in a different direction.

**Instructor:**   Can you notice how fragmented this discussion is? Nobody is following anyone else's line of thought. I think that Gail must feel pulled in six different directions, as she does when she is with Joan. It is as if we were playing out the client's role and Gail has to deal with *us* now.

**Gail:**   That's true; that is just the way I was feeling. I would like to concentrate for a while on the question of seeing her more often than once a week.

**Instructor:**   How do you feel about it?

**Gail:**   Mixed, very mixed. I really get a boot out of some of this stuff. She's funny. I don't know if I've given you the flavor of that or not, but she makes jokes a lot and I laugh and she laughs and she's glad I caught the joke. She comes on as a little girl, a very tiny little girl who needs to be taken care of. She elicits a lot of "Let me take care of you" from me. I think I'm worried about the dependency that she's already started into. For instance, she came one day to the agency and sat for hours on the front steps, although she could have found out that I don't come in on that day. She didn't ask the receptionist. I think there's a hidden question in some of the things she does that says, "How far will you go to take care of me? To what lengths would you go?" I think that scares me.

**Instructor:** It could with good reason. Is that the negative side of the mixed feelings?

**Gail:** There's always a question in my mind about whether it's the best thing for her to be seeing me.

**Instructor:** We have to ask what alternatives there are.

**Gail:** Well, I don't really think there is a better one.

**Instructor:** Then we need to ask why the question persists with you as to whether you should see her.

**Gail:** I think it has to do with—well, I'm intrigued with her. I think she's very interesting. I think I'd learn a lot. On the other hand, because I'd learn a lot doesn't mean that she would get anything out of it.

**Carl:** Are you questioning your competency?

**Gail:** Sure I am. I haven't had anybody come down the pike like this. It will be all new to me. Is it fair to her to essentially experiment?

**Instructor:** We have to ask again, What are the alternatives?— or perhaps, Who are the alternatives?

**Gail:** Well, the truth is that the people who might do better are all booked up.

**Instructor:** I guess that answers the question, doesn't it? But it doesn't tell why the question persists.

**Gail:** I think I'll be scared the whole time I have this client.

**Instructor:** I should hope so, at least some of the time.

The instructor wants to make an important point here by her rather sharp intervention. She wants Gail and the other students to realize that a certain degree of anxiety in treating severely disturbed clients is inevitable and not at all untherapeutic. Especially in the case of inexperienced therapists, lack of anxiety in such situations would indicate so much defensiveness or denial that progress on the part of the client would scarcely be expected.

**Gail:**    Thanks a lot. One thing that worries me about saying to her that I could see her twice a week is that it might reinforce her craziness. She *can* behave in a rational manner, and she has gotten through her courses and gotten good marks, so she can do it. If I said that we've got to meet twice a week, her conclusion would be that she is crazy.

**Instructor:**    I think if you are going to do it, it would be important to do it at a time that makes sense to her and isn't, as you say, a reinforcement of her craziness and isn't a message to her that she can't manage. It should be a message to the effect that "We're doing some important work here right now and it would be good if we could continue that more intensively." You would want to be careful about the timing when you bring it up.

**Gail:**    Yes, I see. I could do that.

Gail has now been reassured that she *should* do what she wanted to do, namely, see the client more frequently.

**Doug:**    I'd like to ask about those stories she brought in for you to read. When you told about that you said, "We went on and on," which sounded as if you thought it was too much, and not really work.

**Gail:**    It wasn't work. I could have stopped at the first one. They were just a few pages each.

**Instructor:**    You might take one as a starting point to get into what is ailing her right now. You mentioned that they all had to do with lonely, isolated people. You might say that this is what you see in the story and ask if that is the way it is with her right now.

**Gail:**    I did do something like that and she acted as if I were criticizing her writing style and flipped over the page to another one.

**Instructor:** There was some real emotion in that, I take it, when she flipped the page?

**Gail:** I don't know whether to call it real emotion. She just shuts you off, that's all.

**Instructor:** I think you have to watch the techniques she has for jumping away from anything touchy. You can't expect literal truth from her, but you can begin to watch what is making her anxious right in the hour. At certain points she moves away from you or shuts you off, as you say. Is that right?

**Gail:** Yes.

**Instructor:** This is the kind of thing you can deal with and hold on to where both you and she have a sense of something real happening that you can both notice. It actually happened. You both saw it.

**Gail:** Yes, I think I see. Like the other day she said, "Do you mind that your office doesn't have any windows?" Before I could get a word out she had apparently changed the subject and moved away. She said, "You know, I never ask anyone any questions." I was somewhat taken aback and didn't know what to say, but she moved on and changed the subject again, so I didn't say anything.

**Instructor:** Don't misunderstand me. I don't mean to try to catch her out in an untruth.

**Gail:** No, I think I understand, but I do have a question about reinforcing her craziness. I think that might be a temptation for me.

**Instructor:** I think this is important to look at. How does it come about that this is a temptation—not only for you, but perhaps for others, too, to reinforce, as you call it, the craziness?

**Gail:** I see her as a puzzle that I don't fully understand, and I listen to these productions of hers and try to figure it out.

**Allan:** That can be frustrating.

**Gail:** Yes, but they're interesting, too, and I find myself trying to put the bits and pieces of all this weird stuff together. I could be far more interested in her tales of big spiders and plants that eat you up than in some of her more reality-oriented statements. She could easily get the impression that I'm more interested in this than in hearing what she does in her daily life. The payoff for me would be to really figure out what all these symbols mean and how they fit together.

**Ellen:**   To figure it out or to fix it?

**Gail:**   Both, I think. But figuring it out is the first thing. It's a game.

**Ellen:**   It's a language.

**Instructor:**   I was just thinking it might be helpful to remember one of the things that Frieda Fromm-Reichmann told about her work with a psychotic man. She followed him around, climbing over the furniture and squatting on the floor and talking the way he did, and finally she said, "I have tried for a long time to speak your language and understand it, and now how about your trying to understand and speak mine?" You needn't do just that with this girl, but I think the principle is appropriate. You do, in a way, have to go into her world to understand it, but you do it so that she can come back into yours, in a more firmly grounded reality. But let's return to what you said about the temptation.

**Gail:**   I think the question I'm asking is, What is best for her right now, and is my being intrigued with the puzzle she presents getting in the way of what is best for her?

**Instructor:**   As Doug mentioned, I think it was a bit of a give-away when you said, "We went on and on," when you were talking about looking at her stories. It indicated that you yourself were not satisfied with what you were doing then.

**Gail:**   Yes, I was concerned about it at the time.

**Harriet:**   I wonder why you did it—let it go on, I mean.

**Ellen:**   When you get caught up like that in trying to figure things out, you've stopped being a therapist for the time being and become a diagnostician.

**Doug:**   You're engaged in intellectual speculation.

**Gail:**   Right.

**Instructor:**   Well, you have to do some of that when you are a therapist, but when you find yourself getting lost in it, perhaps you're using it as a defense.

**Gail:**   Yes, and there was another level that I didn't dwell on. It was, in a way, like a kindergarten child bringing you pictures he's drawn. I think, when a young child does that, he really wants to know whether you like what he did, whether you like his production, and that is the way it was with her.

**Doug:**   So you're being a mommy.

**Fran:**   Is that untherapeutic?

**Instructor:**   I think there is some mothering in a therapeutic relationship, but you want to try to bring insight into the situation, too.

**Gail:**   I tried to do that in telling her that I thought she wanted me to understand her and the stories might help.

**Ellen:**   Only the danger is that next week maybe she'll have to find something else to bring so that you'll understand her, instead of just bringing herself directly.

The discussion is no longer fragmented. People are following each other's thoughts. The instructor is more active than usual, partly because she feels the need to teach, since most of the seminar members have had no experience with clients of this kind, partly because she feels the need to hold the discussion together.

**Instructor:**   I think this brings us back to the theme of reinforcing the craziness. It isn't just craziness. It's presenting you with some kind of far-out production that you are tempted to get caught up in. Then the thing she brings can become not a bridge to greater understanding but a screen to keep you out. And your temptation is to get caught in an intellectual game of making a brilliant formulation. Can you see what the meaning of this game is for you?

**Gail:** I think I'm beginning to see—and I started to say it before, but I didn't see how it fitted in. It's that to make a brilliant formulation would prove that I'm a good therapist. It would relieve my mind that it is really all right for me to work with this girl. Lurking down underneath is always the fear that it's not.

**Fran:** That's quite a fear.

**Instructor:** I think it is potentially there in all of us, this fear of incompetence. When you do puzzle-solving very brilliantly, then you don't have to think about whether or not you are failing with this person as a human being. But this fear comes and goes. If it were there all the time, I think we'd get out of the business.

**Gail:** It does come and go, but it's now more coming than going.

**Instructor:** With this girl particularly?

**Gail:** Right.

**Instructor:** It is quite understandable that a schizoid girl like this, who is on the borderline of being psychotic and is so very anxious herself, would make you anxious in turn.

**Gail:** Yes, I'm thinking back to what you said earlier that this is what she does to me. She confuses me, and then I sound confusing here. I can experience this when I talk about her, and I'm sitting here feeling this way right now.

**Instructor:** Yes, surely. You can think of it as an expression of how lost this girl is in the world of interpersonal relationships. She is confused and can't find her way. She doesn't know how to be with you or with anyone and that makes the session very difficult for you, too.

**Gail:**   I guess this is why she brings in the stories and all this crazy stuff and her weird fantasies.

**Instructor:**   Her threshold for anxiety is much lower than for most of us, so she constantly has to do something to try to get away from it.

**Gail:**   It's not an easy job, but I guess I do want to do it.

Gail has a hard road ahead with this client, but she has gained some sense of what she wants to do with her and feels that she can proceed.

A few months later, Gail is once more presenting Joan, who has made some significant improvement. Her school work is steadier, and she is somewhat better able to work on specific problems in the therapeutic sessions. This time the seminar discussion is not fragmented. It focuses successfully on Joan's troubled relationship with a boyfriend. This is very different from the first presentation, in which the problem was essentially to establish some meaningful communication between therapist and client. The present difficulty is one that bothers many therapists. The client presents a problematic relationship, and the therapist cannot understand what the glue is that holds the relationship together, since it seems to be nothing but a source of misery. Therapists are often baffled by the constant complaints of their clients over a situation from which they could easily extricate themselves. It is tempting to fall into the clients' ways of thinking, to sympathize with them in feeling ill-treated, to advise them to stand up for themselves, and to fail to see what function the relationship serves for them. Gail is, to some extent, caught in this spider web at the beginning of the session. The excerpt centers around this problem.

**Gail:**   Joan is very willing now to answer quite clearly any question I ask, but when she starts talking spontaneously it is hard to get her to be specific. She tells me that she can't remember things, and a lot of the time her facial expression contradicts what she is saying. She's been better about all that, though, since I've brought it to her attention. She has a lot of problems with friends and the way they treat her. She's very concerned that she shouldn't appear selfish in her relationships, but probably, as a result, a lot of people take advantage of her. Instead of confronting them, she gets very angry inside herself. She can't tell them off. But these supposed friends don't seem very important to her. There's only one person who is.

**Instructor:** Who is that?

**Gail:** The boyfriend she is seeing, a guy named Joe. After she told about him, she started talking about having nightmares. She said she kept imagining that she was being watched by a scary-looking person whenever she was by herself. She couldn't get rid of him, and his presence frightened her, especially at night when she would be going to sleep.

**Instructor:** And it's a "he"?

**Gail:** Yes, I forgot to mention that she apparently had several imaginary friends while she was growing up, and she told me they kept her from being alone a lot. But they were never frightening to her.

**Doug:** What does she say about her relationship with this fellow Joe?

**Gail:** She keeps saying that he is her only real friend, but she never says anything positive about him. She sees him as being a lot like her uncle, who was her substitute father. This kind of puzzles me. The biggest thing he does that really gets to her is that he expects her to ask him permission to do things all the time, like her uncle. But he will never talk to her. That's again like her uncle. He is very demanding, intolerant, tyrannical. She says she hates being told what to do and she tries to ignore this quality in him. I had decided to ask her to bring him to the next session and she had agreed, but he didn't show up. He had spent the previous night with her and had practically scared her to death by pretending to be the scary-looking person she sees in her nightmares or daydreams or whatever they are. She doesn't know why he would want to scare her like that, but anyway he decided not to come with her to the session.

**Carl:**   How did it end? Did he stop finally?

**Gail:**   Apparently she started crying and tried to run away. Then he stopped, and I think he apologized. Anyway that's my memory of it.

**Ellen:**   What happened afterward with the two of them?

**Gail:**   Immediately afterward? I really don't know.

**Instructor:**   Well, the lack of information is interesting, too. Have you had any other contact with Joe?

**Gail:**   Yes. This is one of the things I want to talk about. Two sessions later they came in together without any notice to me ahead of time. She was very different when he was there. It was dramatic to see the changes in her. When he was there, she seemed to be trying to be an adult. Then, all of a sudden, she started behaving again like a little child and acting crazy, too. That really scared me. Joe said he didn't feel she was really trying to work out her problems and, if I couldn't do more for her than I had been doing, it was going to be a waste of everybody's time. At that point she started talking about friends whom she had created in her imagination. Her behavior got very bizarre, and I wasn't sure what it was all about. Then Joe said, "Why are you pretending to act so strange? You don't have to." And she got very defensive.

**Fran:**   Is that the first time he has confronted her?

**Gail:**   I don't know. That's the first time I had seen them together. It was scary for me. I said that I was getting very frustrated with what was happening. Joe said they frustrated each other a lot. She said she really wants to work with me in therapy; she wants to work on the nightmares that frighten her a lot. She added that she used to dream as a child but never got so frightened as she does now. Her friends were nicer then. I didn't know whether she meant real or imaginary friends.

Several days later Joe came to my office quite upset. He demanded to see me and claimed that Joan was the most important thing in his life. He couldn't stand to see her so confused and feeling so low about herself. He said he was frustrated because he couldn't find any way to help her and that he had frightened her that night in the hope that she would try harder to help herself. He said he would never desert her, even though he feared she might never improve. I think she's afraid, too, that she'll never get really better. Joe went on to say that he thinks she is worse and he is upset because she is not getting the kind of help she needs. He came to me because now I am the only person he could turn to. I couldn't decide whether I was being insulted or complimented.

**Ellen:**   It sounds almost as though he is in competition for you.

**Harriet:**   Or *with* you for her.

**Gail:**   And she feels very intensely about me now. I really think she is stronger than she was, but that's only when she's not with him.

**Instructor:**   Do you want to formulate a particular question for us to discuss?

**Gail:**   I'm not sure what is really going on between the two of them and why they stay together. I'd like to find some way to make their relationship a little more healthy.

**Allan:**   It was said earlier that a split in their relationship might be dangerous if it happened before she was able to be more independent. I've been feeling that this man, Joe, reinforces some tremendous need she has and it is too hard to break it off.

**Instructor:**   Unless something else were to become more important—such as your relationship to her, Gail. I think you are probably a threat to Joe.

**Fran:**   I think I'd get a little scared if they broke up. What would Joe do to the therapist or to Joan? When he came in demanding to see you in your office, I saw this as threatening.

**Instructor:**   What would you imagine that he might do?

**Gail:**   My fantasy was that he might again try to frighten her, the way he had done before.

**Harriet:**    That is what I saw. Like being again that frightening person in her dreams.

**Ellen:**    I thought he might try to frighten you, too, Gail.

     Seminar members are caught up in the frightening aspects of Joe and of the client's relationship to him. They are fascinated by this and are not addressing themselves to the question of what holds the relationship together.

**Instructor:**    I don't think it's likely that anyone will break off. I think what's important is to try as best you can to get into Joan's head some understanding of how she is keeping up this crazy relationship and for what. Could you help her to see that she has a role and a responsibility in it and that she is using him for something?

**Gail:**    She says he wants her to change, to be something different from what she is. Does she need him for that?

**Instructor:**    I would question whether he wants her to change. What does that mean to her?

**Gail:**    Her question is, "So why do I have to become something different for him to like me?"

**Carl:**    I wonder what "different" means.

**Instructor:**    The presumption is that he is trying to help her. That's the overt statement, isn't it? That's what his visit to your office is supposed to say—"I'm trying to help her and I get frustrated when I can't." But I think all of us have some grave doubts about this. I think it is important for you to keep your eye on *her* responsibility and to show her that it is she who is keeping up this relationship, and to point up to her how crazy she became when he came with her during that one session.

**Allan:**    I wonder if maybe she wasn't behaving appropriately in some of her crazy behavior.

**Gail:**    Adaptively perhaps.

**Instructor:**    But who is making her stay in a situation in which it is adaptive to be crazy? She is. Why?

**Gail:**  He fills some need for her, but she also hates him, I guess.

**Doug:**  It comes as quite a shock to her that there are any alternatives. It's like her friends who make her angry by taking advantage of her. She doesn't have to put up with it, but it never occurred to her that she might make some other friends who would treat her better. She doesn't do anything about it but just keeps talking about how mean they are and how she wishes she could tell them off.

**Instructor:**  This young man, Joe, in a way is not the problem, although she keeps telling you that he is. She is not seeing where *her* power in the relationship comes in. She's putting all the power and all the evil in him when she tells you all the terrible things he does to her. And as Doug said, that's what she does to a lesser extent with her friends as well. That's a very useful role they play, and particularly Joe. It's very nice to have somebody you can put it all on. As long as she needs it that way, she'll have it. It keeps her the poor innocent crazy little girl. This is what she acted out in front of you.

**Gail:**  Oh, yes, I see. That is true. I think she puts all the sex in him, too, and that is evil also. I'm not sure whether they have actually gone to bed together or not.

     Here Gail has a real "Aha experience." She not only perceives the way Joan is projecting her destructive impulses on Joe, which she had not seen before, but she is also able to build on this insight and to bring in the whole area of sex, which had been an unexplored area with this client.

**Instructor:**  I wonder what stops you from asking her about their sexual relationship?

**Gail:**  I have asked myself that and haven't found an answer. Maybe I'm not doing this right with her. I mostly just take what she gives me and don't push much further.

**Ellen:**  I'm interested in hearing why it was difficult for you to ask about their sexual relationship.

**Gail:**    What comes to mind is that she often says that you have to be very careful what you say to people. She doesn't want to say anything that might sound bad. I think probably sex sounds bad, and I think I've been caught up in her standards and didn't want to go into it. Also I think that some time ago she made some passing statement that I interpreted to mean that she was a virgin.

**Instructor:**    It could have been true then and not now. Or it could be that she couldn't speak the truth then, but could now. It may not be so terribly important to pin down what is going on sexually, but she may now be picking up the anxiety from you that you originally picked up from her—that this is a bad subject and not to be talked about. Certainly there are several indications that this relationship with Joe is very intense. The way he frightened her by acting out the scary person of her dreams sounds as if there were something sexual.

**Gail:**    I think I see her now as a seven- or eight-year-old. She seemed about three when she first came in. Somehow you don't bring up sexual relations with a seven-year-old.

**Harriet:**    I don't know about that. Some seven-year-olds are very interested.

**Instructor:**    I would be inclined to think that one of the things you could do with her usefully is to focus on the contradiction between her complaining about all the terrible things Joe does, and, on the other hand, her holding on to him for dear life. If a person were truly rational and he had nothing but complaints about another person, he would leave. Obviously she, like all of us, is not fully rational. But you could just keep questioning what his function is for her.

The instructor has returned to Gail's original question to underline the learning that has taken place. Although Gail herself has seen the point clearly, not all of the other seminar members have yet caught up with her. The difficulty seems to be their unfamiliarity with the mechanism of projection. The students are not yet at home with the idea that one may need a repository outside oneself for one's unacceptable impulses.

**Allan:** She would say that she doesn't want to hurt him, that he needs her, that she has to be careful of him, or something like that, wouldn't she?

**Gail:** Yes, her illusion is that she is all kind and the others are all mean. But she is really very busily making him terribly jealous, now that I think of it. She teases him with her imaginary friends and also with an occasional man who may also be imaginary who calls her up and wants to date.

**Carl:** Perhaps that is some indication of her breaking out of the relationship at least a little.

**Harriet:** Maybe that's why he came to see you. He was threatened by the imaginary friends and maybe some potential real ones.

**Instructor:** So she is teasing the life out of him. That's how much she doesn't want to hurt him.

**Harriet:** I wonder how many million other things she does and how many other people she drives nuts.

**Instructor:** Well, Gail is being driven a little bit nuts, though she is standing up under it very well.

**Doug:** I wonder if she drove her uncle nuts.

**Instructor:** I would suppose so and that could be very exciting, sexually very exciting.

**Ellen:** It's kind of overwhelming, the whole thing. More power to you, Gail!

After this session, Gail continued seeing Joan for some time and was able to help her to maintain herself with adequate grades in college and to acquire some perspective on her relationship with Joe.

The seminar members learned through Gail's presentations to be prepared for some of the difficulties that borderline clients present. There were management questions about whether to see the client at all and, if so, how often. There were questions about getting in touch with her relatives and what to do about the productions that the client brought in to show the therapist. Joe, the client's boyfriend, appeared not only as someone one heard about but also, unexpectedly, in person. Gail found that making clever formulations alleviated her anxiety about whether or not she was competent to deal with Joan's craziness but did not do much to help her client. The seminar as a whole became aware of the phenomenon of "mirroring," which they had engaged in quite unwittingly. They learned to look for this phenomenon and to use their own responses in the seminar as possible indications of what was occurring in the client-therapist interaction.

# CHAPTER 6

# FEAR OF INCOMPETENCE: VERBAL ASSAULTS ON THE THERAPIST

**B**eginning thera-
pists who report feeling very self-confident in their work are
often operating on the basis of strong defenses, particularly
denial. They are not likely to learn anything unless the defenses
can be dropped. The more usual and more hopeful case is that
of the student who easily becomes vulnerable and who feels
insecure about what he is doing. This, however, presents a prob-

lem for both him and his client. In the following sessions, Gail struggles again with this common problem. She is presenting a male client, age thirty-five, who has his Ph.D. in mathematical physics. She has seen him only once. Just before this excerpt she had given his history.

**Gail:**    So he came with two presenting problems, one of which was that he needed help in clarifying a vocational decision. He doesn't know whether he wants to continue in an academic career or whether he wants to do something more practical, more on the applied side. The other one is that he has a social adjustment problem. He formulated it as having had only very little dating experience. He refused to be recorded for the social problem, but wanted it for the vocational problem. For most of the session he didn't look at me. His eyes flitted around the room. It was really difficult to make contact with him.

**Harriet:**    Did you say he had some dating experience?

**Gail:**    Just a little, not much. There were few available girls where he was living before he came here, or so he said. Most of the people were young married couples. I asked him how it had been in college and graduate school, and he said, "I'm sure the other kids I went to high school or college with are married by now."

**Carl:**    Has he had any homosexual experience?

**Gail:**    I didn't get to that point. He was very tense. After some time I commented on that, and then he settled down and started looking at me and talking in a little more relaxed way.

**Instructor:**    I think it's important to notice how often it does have an immediate therapeutic effect if you comment on what you see going on at the moment. That little bit of mutual awareness often changes the situation. Of course, if you do it too abruptly, it may put the client off.

**Gail:**    I asked him if it was characteristic of him to be as anxious as he was in this situation. He said he guessed it was. Then he went into the stories of his last three girlfriends.

**Fran:**   You said "this situation." Did you mean the situation of talking with a female?

**Gail:**   Yes. He's trying to choose a life style. I don't know if you want me to go into the details of these last three girls. I'm not even sure if I remember them all; but in each case it turned out that he felt the girls were using him because they had one or two dates with him and afterwards they got engaged to somebody they had already been going out with. He felt that they were using him to make the real boyfriend jealous or something like that.

**Ellen:**   It's possible that that was true.

**Gail:**   I tried to get from him how it made him feel to have these girls use him. Maybe that's not a good word.

**Instructor:**   Is it the word he used?

**Gail:**   I *think* it's his word.

**Instructor:**   You're not sure?

**Gail:**   No, I'm not sure. He wasn't letting me record, and I'm used to depending on the recording, so I don't remember.

**Instructor:**   That's one of the disadvantages of recording. One gets to depend on it, and one may not listen and remember so well.

**Bob:**   Did you say he had been teaching?

**Gail:**   Yes, in a university in the Middle West. While he was teaching there he took a course in psychology, and he used a lot of words like *ego, superego, social adjustment,* etc. I had to ask him what he meant by *social adjustment*, and it took a long time to get it out of him. I had the impression he had rehearsed a statement, and if I interrupted him, he lost track of where he was. He's a very fearful guy, very defensive and distant, and I really don't know what's going to happen in the sessions.

**Harriet:**   You have two problems to work on, he told you.

**Gail:**   I'm not going to do the vocational one. I'm referring him to another agency for that.

**Carl:**   So he feels the two problems are separate, not related? Did he discuss friends?

**Gail:**   No, he was late, for one thing, and I quit right on time. I had somebody else coming, so it was probably only about forty minutes.

**Instructor:**   I think it's a good idea to quit right on time anyway, even if you don't have somebody else coming in, because you establish that you're here for the time that you have contracted for, and not for more nor less. Another time you *will* have somebody coming in, or you'll have something you need to do, and you get caught in inconsistency about it if you don't do it always the same way. It's a good idea to establish your time boundaries. It goes along with establishing the boundaries of your professional function altogether.

**Gail:**   Yes, I really need that with him. I felt very uneasy. I had another client right after him, and the difference in the way they made me feel was quite astounding. This guy really puts you on. He really is a pretty hostile guy, accusing you of various things—not really accusing, but you feel this is underlying everything.

**Instructor:**   What would he be accusing you of?

**Gail:**   I'm trying to think what I meant and where I got that. I told him I was getting supervision and he was concerned about the credentials of the place.

**Instructor:**   Of the total place?

**Gail:**   Of the total place, and me in it, and the tape recording and what use would be made of that.

**Instructor:**   How did you react, in your own head, to this concern about credentials?

**Gail:**   He had read the statement given him by the secretary about confidentiality, and he knew it almost by heart by the time I got there. I think he had come in another time before this.

**Instructor:**   Did you notice that you didn't answer my question?

**Gail:**   No, I didn't. What was it?

It has taken Gail quite a long time in her presentation to come out with one of her most troublesome concerns, namely, her own lack of experience and "credentials." Having done so, she is not eager to go into it. The instructor wants to call attention to the avoidance of the topic as an indication that there is trouble here, not only for Gail, but for all the seminar members.

**Fran:**   (To the instructor.) You asked for additional information, didn't you?

**Instructor:**   Well, I asked how Gail reacted to his concern about credentials.

**Gail:**   I was a little defensive about it. He's not just somebody you easily warm up to.

**Harriet:**   Do you think that being a woman, after what he said about his experiences with his girlfriends, made you feel insecure?

**Gail:**   Yes, I think at one point I caught myself trying to—well, it went by fast in my mind that this guy is scared to death of women and I think I started trying to be mama for him for a minute, which is kind of silly.

**Instructor:**   These are important things to note, the things that go by fast through your mind. They give important clues to what is going on. Never mind if it seems silly.

**Ellen:**   Being mama was what you were doing with that other client of yours, the one named Mary.

Gail has again skittered off the question of her professional competence. She is on a related and important subject, but is avoiding the one she had touched on. Other members of the seminar collude in the avoidance. They talk for a while about problems related to the client, Mary, who had been presented at an earlier session. They also talk about Harriet's clients, Helen and Nancy (see Chapter Three, Section 2), and note that playing a comforting, supportive role, associated traditionally with mothering, is a pleasant task and one that the female seminar members fall into with especial ease. The men, too, enjoy this role, which is sometimes quite appropriate for a client in deep distress.

**Doug:**    Playing mama is often a trap, though. You get caught in it, and you can't get out.

**Fran:**    The trouble is you can't carry it through. You can't take the client home and feed him and put him to bed. At least you don't usually really want to.

**Allan:**    Well, fortunately, the clients usually don't really want it either, even though they may think they do.

**Ellen:**    Yes, I used to fantasize how wonderful it would be if my analyst would take me home as his little girl. But the truth is I would have hated it after two hours.

**Harriet:**    Sometimes it would be nice, though. I think we're comforting ourselves when we say *they* don't really want it. The truth is *we're* not up to it.

**Allan:**    Well, often both things are true. They don't want it, and they don't need it either. Most of the clients we see can manage quite well for themselves. We would be doing them a disservice not to recognize that.

**Instructor:**    To come back to Gail's client, tell us a little more about his asking for your credentials and what that did to you. What do you feel about it yourselves, the rest of you, if you go to a therapist? Some of you have been in therapy, and others have thought about it. What are your own attitudes?

**Doug:**    I guess before I know somebody, the only guarantee I have is that he has the right degree. Of course, it's not really a guarantee, just a kind of outward something.

**Allan:**    Sight unseen, I look at the credentials.

**Instructor:**    Of course you do.

**Bob:**    But it threatens the hell out of us when other people do it to us.

**Fran:** But isn't it very sensible? Do we want them to go to see some quack?

**Carl:** Maybe when we have our degrees it will be better.

**Instructor:** A person can have all the credentials and accreditation in the world and not be the person for you or not really be a good therapist, but it's a kind of minimal security, isn't it, for the client? It's interesting that we feel it's a bad thing when a client questions us about this, but we would all do it ourselves, perhaps more discreetly than this man did.

**Gail:** Yes, I felt it was undermining me. I think I just feel insecure about whether I am a good therapist, about whether I should be in this field at all, so any little thing that comes along brings that up in me. That's what he did.

Having received some support, Gail is now able to speak out unequivocally about the problem and to see that the client touched on a sore point that she shares with the rest of the seminar.

**Instructor:** How could you use this vulnerability? I don't mean use it in anything you say to the client necessarily, but how could you use it in thinking about him, in the service of your therapy with him?

**Ellen:** Use your own insecurity, you mean?

**Instructor:** Yes. What light might it throw on what is going on?

**Allan:** What was that question again?

Allan has voiced the difficulty all the seminar members are having in staying with the topic. They find it hard to take in the idea of using their insecurity. For the next few minutes they circle around the point without being able to focus on it. Finally the instructor breaks in again.

**Instructor:** I think the insecurity this patient stirs up in you would be stirred up in a lot of people, even if they had all the degrees and all the credentials in the world. In the first hour he made Gail quite uncomfortable and unsure of herself, and she has told us how different she felt with the next client.

**Ellen:**   Maybe he's using the question of credentials as a sort of weapon.

**Instructor:**   Assuming that what is going on is a battle, you would naturally want to have the best weapons you could get, and you would want to disarm your enemy, wouldn't you?

**Gail:**   That is the way I felt it was with him, that he was out to disarm and undermine me. At the same time I had the distinct impression that he was scared out of his mind while he was questioning me.

**Carl:**   That figures. I guess I attack, too, when I'm scared.

**Gail:**   So if my chronic anxiety about not being a good enough therapist is stirred up by him, it's an indication of *his* anxiety.

Gail has finally made a crystal clear statement of how her vulnerability is related to the anxiety of the patient. From here on, she is able to focus more and more usefully on the client's problem.

**Instructor:**   Yes, quite. And now you can notice just when and how his anxiety comes and goes. If you become more aware of your own processes, you can also become more aware of his.

**Gail:**   I think his vocational problem *is* related to his social adjustment problem. He doesn't know who he is in either sphere.

**Instructor:**   There is the same insecurity in both, isn't there? And his question is: "Can I do it? Can I do a good job; can I date a girl; can I talk to a therapist?"

**Gail:**   I think that is basically the question. You get a feeling that he is a very lonely person and he doesn't talk to people and check things out.

**Instructor:**   Can you give us an example of how he does talk? It's hard, I know, without a tape.

**Gail:**   He told me he took this course in psychology and that he really understands about these things—I can't even talk like he does—about all the problems in heterosexual relationships, how you try and you get disappointed because you look for an ideal and your expectations are let down. He talked about reality testing and role adjustment difficulties and went on and on.

**Instructor:**    Did you stop him?

**Gail:**    After a while I stopped him and asked, "Just what do you mean?" and he seemed to get panicked because—I thought, anyway—he had a speech prepared and didn't know how to go on if he couldn't make the speech.

**Doug:**    Maybe you were getting close to something that was important to him.

**Instructor:**    You were also challenging his competence in the one thing he thinks he's any good at, namely, putting words or symbols together.

**Gail:**    I thought he was trying to relate to me in this way, using these psychological words because he knows I am a psychologist.

**Instructor:**    Yes, showing you he has some skills in your field, and some competence, but he doesn't believe in that very much himself, really. This is why I think I would be very careful with him. You always walk a tightrope in this business and especially with a client like this. You don't want to let him get away with things that will be to his disadvantage and waste his time. On the other hand, his ability to relate is so fragile that if you start poking in and saying, in one way or another, "That kind of stuff won't go with me," then he may not have anything to fall back on. I think you have to be firm and cautious at the same time, and I think you were.

**Gail:**    I felt awfully confused for ten or fifteen minutes while I was listening to this.

**Instructor:**    He talked steadily? He didn't let you get in?

**Gail:**    I was searching for a place where I could come in. I was trying to find out what he wanted, and I didn't really know what he meant by "the social adjustment problem."

**Instructor:**    But I think you really did know, because you experienced it. Although we would like to know more about his background and more details about his history, you have his major problem right there in the way he related to you.

**Gail:**    I'm wondering if what might be going on is that he is an attacker, and I am concerned that I will not realize what he's doing and how scared he is and I may attack back.

Gail has moved very far beyond her earlier statements and is able to be aware usefully of some of the dangers involved in her work with this client.

**Ellen:**    I think that's terribly important.

**Gail:**    I think that's why I didn't interrupt him sooner, though it might have saved him a little time. I was wondering when I could interrupt and what I should say, and I felt confused.

**Instructor:**    I think you had two questions: first, what was going on between you and the client, and second, how you could make it useful to him. Until you could answer both those questions I would, myself, prefer to be quiet because you're not there to free associate out loud. You're there to be useful to him, and that has to be the criterion for everything that you do and say. Naturally, you can be mistaken, but that's your criterion.

**Ellen:**    It strikes me that your confusion came on the heels of his questioning your credentials and the credentials of the whole agency. So, of course, you couldn't admit to not knowing what was going on. You would be admitting that you were incompetent.

**Instructor:**    It's a paradoxical kind of thing. Your competence in this field lies in large part in becoming aware of your incompetence. I mean by that an awareness both of your real awkwardness, which you are bound to have as beginners, and sometimes later, too, and also your *feelings* of insecurity related to your lack of credentials and experience.

The seminar members were helpful to Gail and to each other in this session. When the person presenting was open about his or her problem, it usually resulted in a collaborative discussion. All the students participated in this one in a lively and undefensive way, bringing their own experience to bear upon Gail's problem. This is not so apparent in the excerpt as it was in reality, since much has been deleted for the sake of focusing on the point.

The therapist's vulnerability does not disappear overnight, however. It was still evident in a brief follow-up report on the same client a month later, in which the discussion began and ended on the problem of tape recording. This often presented a problem for both clients and therapists. The seminar members became well aware of the disadvantages of the tapes, as foreseen in the first session (see Chapter Two). They found it awkward to introduce the matter to clients, especially the suspicious ones. They found themselves self-conscious, knowing that they would be listened to by colleagues and by the instructor. And they thought that the spontaneity of their clients was often impeded. However, with some exceptions, the usefulness of the tapes in the learning process outweighed these disadvantages. Both therapists and clients, by and large, became used to them. But this client proved to be an exception.

In the following excerpt, Gail is still struggling to find a way to work with this quite suspicious and hostile client.

**Gail:**   He said he didn't want to be recorded, so I didn't. But he also said it was okay if my supervisor sat in on the session. I didn't know what to do with that, and, frankly, I don't know what to do with this guy. He seems to think the room is bugged, even though the tape recorder is there and he can see it isn't on. He came in with problems relating to girls, plus an uncertainty about his vocational choice. We had agreed earlier that he would join a vocational interest group, but he decided last session that he wanted to talk about it with me now.

**Harriet:**   My memory is that he wanted to tackle the personal problem first, that it was most important.

**Gail:**   You're right, and now he's saying he feels more pressure about his vocational choice. He is very concerned about how to find out about himself. He suggested that he bring in a list of adjectives that applied to him as a place to start. I rejected this suggestion, and he said "okay."

**Instructor:**   He may need the adjectives because he has so little awareness of himself and it's safer than venturing into a relationship.

**Gail:**   I told him that I thought it would be more useful to discuss what was happening between him and me in the sessions, and he agreed right away, saying he was glad I was a female because he had difficulties relating to girls.

**Instructor:**   You were suggesting that you would discuss what was going on between you and him, instead of looking at a list of adjectives?

**Gail:**   Yes—the here and now.

**Instructor:**   Did you give any explanation about why you would be doing that?

**Gail:**   No, but I just didn't feel that the adjectives would be very productive.

**Instructor:**   I'm inclined to agree, but I'm wondering what he makes of the proposal that you talk about what's going on in the session. I'm not so sure it's clear to him. He agrees too easily. Why would one do that? Do you think he really understood your suggestion?

**Gail:**   I see what you mean. I didn't question his agreement at the time.

Seminar members tended at first to shy away from an investigation of the "here and now" relationships between themselves and their clients. Such investigations were felt to be embarrassing and anxiety-arousing for both client and therapist. However, they soon found out how enlightening such explorations could be and learned to use the microcosm of the therapeutic situation to understand the clients' interpersonal problems generally. But, as so often happens when one learns to use a new tool, one wants to use it on everything, whether it is appropriate or not and whether it has been carefully introduced or not. The instructor wants the seminar members to consider thoughtfully how this kind of exploration may be experienced by a client who has not yet grasped its potential significance.

**Instructor:** I'm talking about the fact that what we take for granted as an ordinary way of proceeding may seem strange to a particular client.

**Allan:** They come in because of this sick relationship with other people, and because the therapist is a person, they develop the same sick relationship with the therapist. Hopefully they can learn to see what is going on and resolve it, which should then generalize to their other relationships.

**Instructor:** That is *our* rationale, but how does it seem to the client?

Allan has learned his lesson well. He voices for the seminar what they have assimilated as "good students." The danger of learning any theory or method lies, of course, in taking its assumptions for granted. It then becomes difficult to look at. Ellen, in her statements that follow, is able to provide a fresh point of view from her own experience.

**Ellen:** I don't think I could have bought that when I first went into therapy.

**Instructor:** That's why I'm asking what this man is buying, and I'm wondering if he hasn't bought it a little too quickly.

**Fran:** One thing that puzzles me: he says he has a problem with girls, but he wants to develop a list of adjectives to talk about instead. It's like he's using therapy not to do anything.

**Gail:** I think I sensed that.

Instructor:    I'm concerned that he agrees *immediately* to discuss what's going on in the session between you and him. As I said, it may make good sense to us, but I'm wondering if it really does to him.

Gail:    He just couldn't define his difficulties. I think this is where he brought up the adjective check list as a way to find out what's going on with him. He wants to know who he is, and he thinks or hopes he can know this by having someone show him his personality profile. He would like to take psychological tests.

Gail, along with other members of the seminar, is quite incapable at this time of staying with the question about her relationship with the client. Again and again she moves away from this point, although she herself has proposed to the client that they study this.

Instructor:    Ellen, could you say a little more about how you couldn't have bought the idea of looking at your relationship to the therapist at the beginning of therapy? It might be helpful to us to hear what you found strange about this.

Ellen:    I had a lot of problems to resolve with other people, especially my parents. I would have thought that the furthest thing removed from what I needed and wanted was what was happening between me and my analyst. I found out soon enough that it was very relevant, but I didn't realize it at the beginning.

Gail:    I see what you mean. This man is confusing because, on the one hand, he is so challenging and suspicious and, on the other hand, he goes along with what I propose when he might well not know what I mean. I think he has tried a lot of different ways of solving his problems, but none of them worked and he's feeling desperate. So it seemed he was willing to try my suggestion, though it may not have made real sense to him.

Instructor:    With a person as suspicious as this man is, I think it might behoove us to be a bit suspicious in return when he agrees so readily.

**Fran:**   What do you feel about him as a person?

**Gail:**   The first time I met him, my defenses went right up. You remember, he challenged my credentials and then he said he wouldn't be recorded. But he talked "psychology" and used such terms as *id* and *ego* as if to say he knew the same things I did. The last session, he brought in a book and asked if I'd read it. I hadn't and I felt challenged again.

**Instructor:**   All of which indicates discomfort and tells us how much trouble he's in.

**Gail:**   I feel sorry for him. His eyes—he looks like a scared rabbit, but he alternately attacks and asks for help. I feel alternately like wanting to mother him and like running away from his attacks. It's not very pleasant to have your client thinking that you're not much good as a therapist. I guess I'd rather mother him and think of him as helpless. When I suggested that we talk about our relationship, I'm not sure I was really so keen to do it. I just thought I ought to do that. When he agreed so fast, I guess I was a little baffled to know what to do next.

   Gail is now opening up with what she had been struggling with. This is not an easy client to deal with, but the seminar has enabled her to be more and more honest and more and more aware of herself in relation to this man.

**Instructor:**   You know, you have been doing a very good job with your client. The fact that he continues to come to see you indicates that. From his history I should think he has no good reason to trust you or anybody else in this world. And here he is letting you in on his troubles, a little more each time he sees you. With regard to the tape recording, I'm not so sure if I were in his place that I would be so eager to be recorded.

**Gail:**   I know *I'm* not, and perhaps that is part of the problem. I can't be just matter-of-fact about it, and I probably communicate some of my hesitation to him, and he has plenty of hesitation of his own.

**Instructor:**   He might want to say all kinds of embarrassing things. And who wants that on tape?

**Gail:**    For myself, I wouldn't want it.

**Harriet:**    I wouldn't either. I find that sometimes I don't say what I would like to say to a client because I'm afraid it will sound foolish when I play the tape, even when I just play it to myself. If I play it to the seminar, it's that much worse.

**Carl:**    Yes, if you stay quiet, at least you haven't said anything dumb.

**Instructor:**    Well, then, you can imagine that the client may have similar feelings. Even if he isn't being graded in a course, he is "on the record" as having revealed himself as stupid or helpless or greedy or any of a million unadmirable things.

**Doug:**    It helps a little bit when you begin to realize that we are all in this together.

Doug has put into words a redeeming feature of the seminar form. To be sure, this sense of being in it together is not always in evidence. But when it is, learning is facilitated and morale is high.

Gail's struggles with this difficult client illustrate how the insecurity of inexperienced therapists can be used in the client's interest if it is admitted into awareness. Students and beginning therapists generally often feel strongly that their lack of accreditation or their lack of the proper degrees is at the root of their difficulties with clients and that all will be solved when they can hang their diplomas on the wall. Although there is some basis in reality for this attitude, it is important to realize, as Gail did in this chapter, that the feelings are more importantly a function of the relationship between her and the client. They are stirred up in a particular way by a kind of anxious attack made by a particular kind of client. It is important for the student to become aware of this. Gail's experience illustrates the importance of being aware of the insecurity that underlies the attack. The client presented is exaggeratedly suspicious about credentials; his own do him very little good in the world of interpersonal relations, in which he finds himself grossly incompetent. The presenting student, Gail, who is quite capable of doing good work with other clients, responds immediately with doubt about her own competence. The discussion about tape recording that engaged several seminar members reflects the general fear that their incompetence will be revealed to each other and to the instructor.

# CHAPTER 7

# TRANSFERENCE
# AND
# COUNTER-
# TRANSFERENCE

Transference and countertransference problems were actually a part of almost every case presentation in the seminar. This chapter emphasizes the special problems in this regard that can arise when a client is seen over a long period of time. In long-term therapy, such problems can become more intense than in shorter term therapy.

In the following four excerpts Ellen presents a client whom she saw twice a week over a period of almost two years. This is a longer time than was usual in the seminar. Although seminar members learned to become aware of their attitudes toward their clients even in very short-term therapy, more extended discussion of their feelings became essential when the therapy became more intensive.

It is assumed that clients will become dependent upon their therapists in intensive psychotherapy and that this dependency should be interpreted and resolved. It is not so acceptable that therapists will become dependent upon their clients for the satisfaction, real or fantasied, of some of their needs and wishes. When it happens, as indeed it does in spite of its unacceptability, it tends to give rise to anxiety, because it is something of which the therapist is not exactly proud. It is not sufficient to point this out only once. Just as a client in therapy must work through a particular self-destructive pattern many times before it loses its hold over him, so the therapist, too, must see his own pattern over and over again before it begins to disappear. It is a matter of allowing growth to take place—always a long-term process requiring patience.

Weeds can be dug out in seconds. And this is comparable to flashes of insight: "Oh, that's what that is. I don't need to do that, do I?" But the growth of a new pattern of life, as of a new art or skill, will not be hurried. It is not surprising, then, that in the following excerpts the theme of dependence of the therapist on the client appears over and over in various forms. In each excerpt some different aspect of the problem becomes visible. Meanwhile, both therapist and client are growing.

The client in this case was a young man in his twenties, called Ben, who was living with his girlfriend and working at a very challenging job in a publishing house. His presenting problem had been his inability to concentrate on his work. This symptom had become so severe when he began therapy that his job was in jeopardy, since he often did not complete assignments on time. He mentioned as a second difficulty the unsatisfactory nature of his relationship to the woman with whom he was living. He was preoccupied with jealous fantasies and with the performance of various compulsive, ritualistic behaviors that interfered both with his work and with his interpersonal relationships.

     Prior to the next excerpt, Ellen had summarized her client's history and the work of earlier sessions. She is now talking about more recent developments. Ben had returned after quite a long break for a business trip. Ellen's voice is much softer than usual; she seemed reluctant to be heard. Seminar members had been leaning forward, straining to catch Ellen's words. They realize that she is uneasy.

**Instructor:**    Are some of you having trouble hearing?

**Ellen:**    Oh, I'm sorry. I'm talking down to my lap. I think there was a lot going on in him in our last session, but I'm not quite sure what it was. He may have been telling me he was glad to be back, but I'm not sure. That's one of the things I want to talk about here, because I want to find out. Then he said he felt comfortable during his therapy sessions, but outside of the sessions he felt less confident about his relationships. I'm not sure what was going on. I'm not sure that I missed the process at this point.

**Instructor:**    I'm not sure that you did, either.

**Ellen:**    Is that what I said? "I'm not sure I missed it?" Wow! What is he saying? And what am I saying?

     Ellen is aware, as are other seminar members, that her slip of the tongue indicates how much is going on outside her awareness. She also has some glimmering of how much she wants to keep the relationship with Ben private. The slip is one more indication of her anxiety.

**Instructor:**    Anybody have any thoughts?

**Allan:**    I thought that when he said he felt comfortable during the therapy sessions he was saying that you and he have a special relationship that he can't find outside.

**Fran:**    It sounded as if he were saying there was no competition in the sessions, that he had you all to himself.

Ellen:    That's part of what I picked up, but not just then.

Harriet:    What I hear from this whole thing is how dependent he is on you. He can't handle the outside world, so as soon as he gets back in town he comes to see you, though before he went on the trip he had thought of stopping.

Ellen:    Yes. Just before this we had talked about dependency.

Fran:    His dependency on you?

Ellen:    Yes, and how hard that was for him. I had been trying to get him to deal with his dependency and this is the first time that he has really come near it.

Instructor:    But you have the funny feeling you missed something?

The seminar is on the track of the problem of dependency, but the members are still concentrating solely on the dependency of the client and are not considering the therapist. The following indicates that Ellen has an idea that the trouble lies in something about her own response to the client.

Ellen:    I wasn't sure whether he was just saying he was glad to be here or whether he was telling me something about me. I think I missed it. I didn't focus on his feeling that he needed me and that he was "glad to be back." I went into an abstract discussion of relationships between people, and I guess I pushed him away.

Ellen illustrates here a frequent occurrence in beginning therapists. She has been made uncomfortable by Ben's dependency, which reminds her of her own, and, rather than staying with this uncomfortable situation, she goes into an abstract discussion.

Gail:    One of the things that occurred to me, but I don't have enough evidence, was that it sounded like a seductive statement.

Ellen:    Which one? From him or from me?

Ellen is again on the track of seeing her own involvement, but in the next statement Gail lets her off the hook; the seminar wanders again for a bit. However, in the wandering there is also some working toward and working through the problem. The longest way round was the shortest way home, as is often the case.

**Gail:**    From him.

**Ellen:**    Yes, I think so. I think I was picking up in a subliminal way that he was being seductive, and I pushed him away.

**Instructor:**    He is doing everything possible to be your only child.

**Ellen:**    Right, he has always wanted that from someone.

**Instructor:**    I think the seduction is not so much sexual. He must have really suffered as a child in having his nose out of joint when his brother arrived on the scene. So, when you felt, as you say, subliminally, that he was trying to seduce you into being mother just for him alone, you made it into an abstract discussion.

**Ellen:**    My favorite thing.

Ellen has become aware of her typical defensive maneuver. It is worth noting that therapists may be aware, in principle, of their own defenses without being able to do without them, but they learn gradually to use the presence of the defense as a sign that they are avoiding something.

**Doug:**    I have the feeling when I listen to you talk about him that he has just sucked you right in there. I would feel like telling him that this is a bunch of crap. I don't know if that's therapeutically right, but I would have trouble sitting there listening to him if he talked like that all the time.

Doug's strong reaction here is an indication of his discomfort in hearing about the intimate relationship between Ellen and Ben. He is one who finds it especially hard to use his own dependent responses to clients in a therapeutic way. His inclination to tell Ben that what he is saying is "a bunch of crap" stems from intolerance of his own dependent tendencies as well as those of clients. Doug is giving voice to an aspect of the seminar group that favors expressing oneself impulsively to get something off one's chest, a maneuver that usually does not speak to the client's problem, but may afford relief to the therapist.

The seminar members are now all looking at the instructor expecting her to pass judgment on the correctness or incorrectness of this kind of intervention. She considers it to be more useful to stay out of the position of judge in this case.

**Instructor:**   It's hard to say what's therapeutically correct when you are not in Ellen's shoes and you're not inside her skin. But I think if you can get in touch with what you are experiencing you can more likely use it therapeutically.

**Gail:**   I feel there's something mutual going on. You've gotten him sucked in as much as he has you. You ask him a nice abstract, general question and he gives you a nice abstract general answer.

**Ellen:**   Yes, pushing each other away. I keep going through the motions of periodically pulling him back and then taking the first opportunity to move away again into the abstract.

Ellen is now being more self-disparaging than is necessary. She has actually done a very workmanlike job with Ben, but from time to time she becomes anxious about her own involvement.

**Instructor:**   I think it would be interesting to find out what in the relationship pushes you into the abstract. He seems to follow where you lead. If we can find out what pushes you, then we can break the cycle.

**Allan:**   My feeling is that you were afraid he would go back to his old rituals that you thought you had helped him out of, and then he'd be in danger of losing his job again. Maybe you were afraid to confront him about some of the things you were feeling, because you were afraid he might get worse.

Allan is representing a side of the seminar that is often apparent. He wants to get in, not having said much during this session. The intervention says more about his own fears than about the present problem. The instructor brings them back.

**Instructor:** I found that your discussion with Ben reminded me of this seminar. We ask ourselves, "Could it be this, or could it be that? Would this or that make a nice hypothesis?" and so forth. And you say something similar to him. I don't mean to say that there is no place in therapy for the presentation of hypotheses, but your discussion was on such a high level of abstraction that I wonder what you are running away from and helping him to run away from.

**Doug:** I would say you were afraid to confront him because you thought he might get worse because of the confronting.

**Allan:** You don't want to be responsible if he gets worse or if he leaves therapy.

Doug is supporting Allan in his hypothesis of what is going on and also keeping Ellen from speaking for herself. It sometimes happened that the male members of the seminar felt that they had to assert themselves against female domination, especially because the instructor was a woman. This was usually outside of awareness and was not sufficiently commented on during the sessions, by the instructor or anyone else.

**Ellen:** I must be dumb, but I don't know what you're talking about. I'm sorry.

Ellen is using the defense of calling herself dumb, which she certainly is not, to avoid telling Doug and Allan that they are off the track and not helping her to get at the trouble.

**Doug:** What I'd really like to hear is a description of a time when he has retreated because of something you did. Would you give an example?

**Ellen:** (In an irritated voice.) I can't give you a concrete example because my head doesn't work that way. I can't remember specific incidents, which is probably why I go into abstractions so easily. But what I'm struggling with now is the memory that when we first met, he would go off into a jungle of intellectualization any time I would attempt a confrontation with him, and I wouldn't be able to do anything. There was nothing I could do but sit and listen.

The direct request for an example flusters Ellen, and she has some difficulty in responding to what sounded like an accusation. She is unaware that she has used the phrase "when we first met," which sounds more like a social situation than a therapist-client relationship, in which one usually says "when he first came to the clinic" or something of the kind. The instructor now tries to get her back to where she might more easily see what she is avoiding.

**Instructor:** You said earlier that when you got up the nerve to mention his failure to say anything about his fantasies concerning you, it broke down a barrier and he was able to talk more freely.

**Ellen:** Yes, we were able to talk better. Did I say "he"? I should say "we." That's true.

**Instructor:** I'm trying to get at what you are concealing from yourself and what you're afraid of. Some people think you are afraid he'll get worse or stop treatment. Do you think that's it?

This is an attempt to clear away an assumption that the instructor feels is not true and that has functioned as a red herring.

**Ellen:** I think his improvement so far is pretty solid, and I also don't think he will stop treatment. I'm sure he won't.

**Gail:** As long as it's a special kind of place with you, as he said, he'll never stop.

**Instructor:** During part of this last session you were not being abstract. He was really telling you where and when it hurt, and then something happened and you both went off. What was it?

**Gail:** It's like—once it got to an intense point, but then, rather than deal with the tension, you did something else instead of holding him there and sticking to it.

(Several seminar members nod their heads in agreement.)

**Ellen:** But we did stick to the issue of dependency almost the entire session.

**Gail:** You were dealing with the same issue but changing the level on which you dealt with it. (Gail speaks with warmth and supportive sympathy.)

**Ellen:** So it's like changing the subject. And I guess I did jump away.

**Instructor:** And what happened in your head just before that? You were dealing with dependency, but . . .

**Ellen:** Oh, whose dependency? All right, I finally got the message.

**Instructor:** Yes, I think that is it.

With the help of the seminar, and particularly with Gail's warm support and the instructor's very specific question, it became possible for Ellen to move into the center of her anxiety. Ellen has come to the point of seeing what she was avoiding—namely, her own dependency. In what follows she was reluctant to do the necessary working through "in public," but the time was not up and the discussion continued.

**Ellen:** I'll have to watch for that. I don't think I have any more to say about it right now.

**Instructor:** Could we ask you how you felt when you stopped with him before he went away on his trip? I think it was left open whether or not he would return to therapy. His symptoms were a lot better.

**Ellen:** I'm trying to remember. I thought at that point that the presenting problem was pretty much alleviated. He was okay on the job and I felt good about that. We had worked out some things together. But I felt there was a great deal in terms of his development as a man that needed to be worked on further. I thought if he stopped then it would be unfortunate, because he would never reach his potential. My fantasy was that if he didn't continue now, he would find after a time that he needed to go on and I hoped he would be able to get somebody at least as good as I was.

**Instructor:**   And somebody else would reap the cream. I know one doesn't "reap" cream, but is that right, in essence?

**Ellen:**   No, I didn't think that. I don't know why I didn't, because it seems as if I would. My fantasy was that he would get somebody as good as I, and maybe I thought of that as myself.

**Instructor:**   Yes, I heard you say "*at least* as good as I" and another phrase you used was "he wouldn't reach his full development as a man" or something like that.

**Ellen:**   Yes, that was it.

**Instructor:**   And you'd miss out on that?

**Ellen:**   I wasn't consciously thinking of that. I don't know what you are asking. Maybe I'm stupid.

Ellen is again disparaging herself, thus avoiding any further investigation of her attitudes. She is not intending to do this, but is responding to the pressure that has been put on her during this session.

**Instructor:**   I will just say what came to my mind. I thought of a mother who sees her son develop into a man with the regret that she will not have the benefit of it. Some other woman will. It's fine that he's going to be a man, but too bad that someone else will have the benefit. I wanted to go a little more deeply into the nature of your dependency on him.

**Ellen:**   Maybe that's the way it is with me. But can I get off the hook now?

**Gail:**   Are you really on the hook?

**Ellen:**   I don't feel personally attacked, but this has been hard.

**Instructor:**   It is hard to be honest. It really is, but that's the work of therapy. Let's stop for today.

About two months later, Ellen presented her client again. After the preceding session she had commented to the instructor that the discussion had been very enlightening to her, but also quite painful. This time she has been presenting in a much more concrete way and has clearly been doing very significant work with the client. The following excerpt is from the end of the seminar.

**Ellen:** He has been telling me more about the fantasies he has that bother him. He imagines a woman betraying her lover with another man. He is the one who is betrayed, and he is furiously angry and jealous. He gets her back, and she feels so guilty that he can get her to do anything he likes. Right after that he said he can never be spontaneous with people because he always has to be in control of what is going on. He always has to maintain an image of himself, and he hopes that others have the same image. He talked about how that was with me. He says he has less need to do that with me than with others, and he kept talking about my professional status; that I couldn't talk about him with others because my professional status would not allow it. I did point out that he didn't need to control me in that respect because I was already controlled by what was permitted and not permitted to a psychologist. He agreed and then said that he would like it if he could push buttons on people like on a Coke machine and get what he wanted to come out! The next session he went off into a long, intellectualized discussion on a whole series of items. And I was sitting there getting angry. I tried to get in touch with what was making me angry, and it seemed to me it was that he was treating me like a Coke machine or a computer. He brought in this program that he was feeding into me, and I was supposed to come out with the answer. So I told him I felt like I might as well be a computer and that he was pushing me away. The wall was beginning to come up between us again. I said he must do this to others too.

Ellen seems to have made very good use of what she had learned. She has noted her anger, found its source, and been able to put it to her client in a way that he can hear.

**Ellen:** He seemed to get some insight from this. He said he guessed he did this with his girl and that she then ignores him, and he said he would watch for it; I supported him in this. The next time he came in very depressed. He talked about feeling completely defenseless.

**Carl:**   I hope you said you only wished it were true.

**Ellen:**   No, I didn't. He was speaking very intensely, and I didn't want to put him down. He talked the whole session about wanting to reach out and really touch people and not just program them. When he left he went out of the door and then suddenly came back and put his hand on my shoulder, which took me quite by surprise.

The next session he was feeling better. He said he had wanted to touch me several times during the session but was afraid he would deceive himself about his feelings, and then on the way out it just overpowered him and he didn't even think about control. He felt like thanking me and didn't mind now admitting that he needed help. Then he went back to the fantasy and how it controls him and that meant it was a compulsion, and he asked me if he could ever get over a compulsion. He said it had such a hold on him and it causes such disruption in his life with his girl, even in their sexual life.

**Instructor:**   Could it be the other way around? That his life, sexual and otherwise, with his girl is disrupted and one of the things that happens is that he becomes preoccupied in an obsessive way with fantasies rather than with the real relationship?

**Doug:**   Maybe fantasies are part of a repertoire he developed at age two to solve his problems.

Ellen refuses to let herself be sidetracked by the comments and continues along her own way.

**Ellen:**   I was thinking that what bothers him about his fantasies, which he obviously enjoys with one part of himself, is that he can't stop them. *He* is not in command; he is overpowered by them, as he was overpowered by his impulse to touch me. But in the case of touching my shoulder on the way out, it was a way of relating to me in reality. It was not forbidden, and I didn't reprove him or move away. But the fantasies are unacceptable to him because he can't stop or even start them at will. He can't keep up the image of himself as the one in control, even though in the content of the fantasies, he *is* the one in control. It's very hard to explain. I was thinking all these things and what I found myself doing was going off into a lecture on responsibility, all about how everyone is responsible for what he does and thinks even when he is overpowered by an impulse or a fantasy. He sat back and said "Uh-huh" in an indifferent kind of way and I knew I had lost him.

**Instructor:**    Is that why you didn't bring the tape of that session today?

**Ellen:**    Yes, I think I handled it there pretty clumsily, and anyway it's a bad tape.

**Instructor:**    You surely want to ask yourself what is the anxiety behind handling it clumsily. You were doing a very good job, and then you became clumsy, so we have a puzzle. But unfortunately the time is up. Maybe you could think about it.

It is not far afield to speculate that Ellen has been thrown off by the anxiety that *she* might not be in control of the situation with the client. His touching her had in itself been harmless enough, but it brought home to her that he might do other things that she would not be able to stop. The fear of losing control in the therapeutic relationship masks the unacceptable desire to let the client control her as he does the woman in the fantasy. In order to remain "therapist" she goes into a lecture on responsibility, which is aimed at herself and misses the mark with the client. She is dealing with a very anxiety-provoking situation and with a very complex client. It may be just as well that she gives herself and the client a rest at this point, before going any more deeply into what is troubling them both.

A few weeks later, Ellen presents again and goes further with the problem of her involvement with Ben. She refers to the last time she had presented and to the lecture she had given on responsibility.

**Ellen:**    I think what I was busy doing at that point and what he was busy doing with the ten minutes left in the session was reducing his anxiety a little bit. I should say "our anxiety," my anxiety too. The next time he came in quite anxious again and I did something different. I tried to remind him that once before he had been anxious in the session, and he had got through it by just sitting in it and hanging on without trying to do anything about it. He could see that he was going to have to do that again, but he didn't feel hopeless this time.

Ellen now summarizes the remaining sessions, which have had their ups and downs.

**Instructor:**   Well, let's see what questions you want to discuss this time.

**Ellen:**   I'm not sure whether I am right in pushing him to deal with me as a sexual being, to try to bring together me as an asexual psychologist and me as a sexual person. He puts it that he is both a spiritual person and a physical person and he can't get the two together. But he doesn't bring me into it.

**Harriet:**   I was thinking that it is difficult to deal with. When you get into the area of sex and the relationship between the two of you, it's hard, because you both have very intense feelings and the problem of control is a real one and not easy. I should think it would be frightening to open up that area between you and him.

**Ellen:**   Maybe so, but I'm less frightened of opening up the issue of his control than I am of thinking about the kinds of cues I might be sending out to him. I think perhaps I was indicating to him nonverbally that I was sexually attracted to him, and he must have felt a question as to what he was going to do about it. What I'm afraid of is my own sexuality. That's where it's at.

The atmosphere of the seminar is such that Ellen can formulate the problem as it seemed to her and expect some help in moving forward with it. At this point, she herself sees no clear way out.

**Gail:**   I've had a similar experience. I had a client and I began feeling countertransference kinds of things, and the whole time I was concerned about my feelings; I almost lost the client.

Gail offers the support of similar fears and similar experiences in a situation that she feels she did not handle well. This is sometimes all that is needed to permit a therapist to do further work with the problem. In this case, the instructor feels called upon to add something, for even in these liberated times therapists often feel strong taboos on their sexual feelings toward clients. It is assumed in this seminar that clients are off limits to therapists so far as sexual or social activity is concerned. This does not necessarily make it easier to be aware of and to deal with the sexual impulses that occur.

**Instructor:** It's interesting that you use the word *counter-transference* when you are referring to sex. It is so forbidden to have sexual feelings toward a client that it is nicer to call it countertransference. Alas, it is just those things that do occur in our fantasies. It is not surprising if Ellen has sexual feelings about this young man. But do you think, Ellen, that either you or he will act on your sexual impulses to each other? Are you afraid of that?

**Ellen:** I asked him that last time. At first he said no and then he thought he might be afraid. I asked him if he didn't sometimes in his mind put his girl in between himself and me so that he wouldn't have to think of me in a sexual way.

Ellen is giving very relevant material here but avoiding the question as it refers to herself.

**Fran:** At least we know you'd like to go to bed with him, but we don't know if he'd like to go to bed with you. Can you come right out and talk about that?

**Ellen:** There's something else involved. There's also the matter of control, as Harriet said.

Ellen is agreeing that Harriet was right, though she had denied it a few minutes earlier. She is also confirming the hypothesis that the really troublesome area for her is her fear of not being in command of herself. It is reasonable to suppose that behind that there is an unconscious desire to give over the control to someone else.

**Harriet:** Why isn't that sex?

**Fran:**   It sounds like it's tied up with that.

**Ellen:**   Yes, it's tied up with sex. What's running through my mind is his fantasy of the woman who was unfaithful and then came back, guiltily willing to do anything her lover wanted.

> Ellen is indicating again her difficulty in dealing with this problem.

**Gail:**   In one of your other presentations you were talking about his relationship with his girl and you said that he insists on her making the advances to him, and the element of who controls whom is very much connected with that. She *seems* to be the one to call the shots, but he makes her do it.

**Ellen:**   Yes, I'm just wondering what the fear is for him.

**Instructor:**   I get the feeling that you are so troubled by your own responses and your own reactions that you can't really keep your eye on him.

**Ellen:**   That's very true. I think what was troubling me was that I don't know what's underneath with me, what kind of messages I'm really allowing to come through to him.

> Ellen is expressing clearly here her sense that she has not yet uncovered what is going on in her own mind. But she is very close to it and is searching in a relatively undefended way that allows the seminar to help her.

**Harriet:**   It sounds as if the messages to him were very seductive, asking him please to make love to you, and even more, please to take you over completely and be there just for you.

**Ellen:**   Yes, I know I'm attracted to him, but I don't have a problem with that, except that it's in a therapy situation.

**Harriet:**   Yes, but that's it. It *is* a therapy situation.

> Ellen has defended herself by admitting part of what Harriet has said with a "Sure, I know that already" attitude, but she overlooks the really critical second part of what Harriet has said.

**Gail:** Have you thought, if you let your wishes run free, would you like to get out of the therapy situation and meet this client somewhere outside?

**Ellen:** I did fantasy that. (She pauses and then speaks slowly and thoughtfully.) I guess that is not really what I'm concerned about. I think I'm more concerned with the message I'm sending, which says: "Don't let anyone else get in here between us. Just let it be you and me, and I want you all for myself. Don't let your girl in here."

**Gail:** (Very supportively.) You're more concerned about your jealousy and possessiveness than about your sexual feelings?

**Ellen:** Yes, I think so. It's the possessiveness. Oh, yes, and that's interesting because what he came up with right before all this was going on was that his girl had said she was very jealous of me.

Ellen has now allowed herself to be aware of how another aspect of what the client had been talking about (his girl's jealousy) fitted the picture. What has happened here is typical of what happened when the seminar was working well. The presenter at first denies and defends herself and then slowly sees that the point that had been made (in this case by Harriet) was correct. In what follows, the instructor brings in an additional point that had not been brought up before.

**Instructor:** Does this have a special importance because, in a couple of months, you will have to terminate with him?

**Ellen:** Yes, definitely.

**Instructor:** And he is going to be turned over then to somebody else, either to the wide world, including his girl, or to another therapist, or both. I think you have mentioned that you had in mind a particular therapist to whom you would like to transfer him, who would then become "another woman."

**Ellen:** Yes, it's the jealousy and possessiveness that I'm really concerned about, not purely sexuality. I've never dealt with this in therapy with a client before.

**Instructor:** You can't deal with it very well until you are aware of it.

**Ellen:** I think I was right on the edge of awareness of it when I was listening to the tape, but I was trying to get away from it. I think that feels very right.

Although Ellen is still troubled by her own feelings, she is relieved and even somewhat satisfied at having identified them in a way that feels "right." She is now in a better position to use her own feelings and attitudes with the client.

What follows does not bring anything new, but it under-lines the learning that had just taken place and allows other seminar members to participate. It is noteworthy that the dis-cussion up to this point had been almost entirely among the women seminar members. It was by no means always the case, but at certain times the women formed a clear subgroup when support seemed to be needed for one of their number. Some-times a pair functioned in this way. The men no doubt felt pushed out at such times and often reasserted themselves, as in the following, against the all-too-evident female domination.

**Allan:** I'm wondering, just out of curiosity, if you terminated with him today, would you rather turn him over to another therapist or not?

**Ellen:** At this point I would rather turn him over to another therapist, because he still has some problems.

**Bob:** That's a rational decision, but I don't think that was the intent of Allan's question.

**Allan:** That's right. I was asking on another level. Just at a gut level, would you rather turn him over to a therapist or to his girl?

**Ellen:** Well, his relationship to his girl is better than it was, but there is still an essential area untouched between them. Yes, on a purely gut level, I would rather turn him over to a therapist than to his girl. The therapist can't really have him any more than I can. Oh, it's terrible to be a human being in here.

**Instructor:**   It's terrible to be a human being anywhere. The seminar just highlights the difficulties.

**Doug:**   I was thinking that, to feel you are effective, you might try various ways to prove yourself and gain a sense of power. If you are sexually attractive to this man, that would be one way. I know I am susceptible to this kind of thing.

(Other seminar members nod in agreement.)

**Ellen:**   Yes, that's tied up in it.

**Instructor:**   I think the hard thing is to be aware of all these less-than-noble impulses we have and at the same time try to use them in the service of the task. You can't do the job unless you are aware of the degree of self-concern that you have in doing this work that is supposed to be for others.

The seminar members have to struggle again and again with this same problem of the self-image of the therapist as a completely selfless character. Beginning therapists often tend either to deny the intensity of their egotistical concerns or to go to the other extreme of self-deprecation, which they frequently want to share with their clients in order to be "honest" and "authentic."

In the fourth and last presentation, termination is close at hand, since Ellen is leaving the agency. As so often happens, the client's old symptoms return with intensity when the therapist is about to leave, and it is almost as if no work had been done at all. Beginning therapists, unfamiliar with this pattern, are often in despair at such times until they can see what is happening and interpret it gently but firmly to the client without too much emotional involvement.

Ellen has summarized the content of the last session, which consisted mainly of talk about sexual problems and memories of childhood.

**Ellen:**   I sat last night trying to formulate a question, and I think I just don't know what is going on. All of a sudden, or so it seems, he is worse. The last time I reported, I became aware of my possessiveness, and it has really helped in working with him. I'm not so much troubled by it. But he doesn't seem to be working with me now. Out of nine scheduled sessions, he missed two and came late to most of the rest.

**Instructor:**   Before we throw it open for general discussion, could I ask what has been said about the lateness and missing the appointments? What does he say about it?

**Ellen:**   He says he is late probably because he doesn't want to talk about some things.

**Instructor:**   What things?

**Ellen:**   Sexual things.

**Instructor:**   But he talked about practically nothing else.

**Ellen:**   I pointed that out.

**Instructor:**   I noticed he said "probably because." If it is just "probably," it means he is finding a rationalization, not actually experiencing something. When he didn't come, did he forget?

**Ellen:**   Oh, no! He has the most esoteric things happen to him on his job that prevent his leaving. Each time it's something else.

**Instructor:**   It would make sense, wouldn't it, that rather than let you abandon him he is leaving you first? It's as if he's telling you, "I'm going away, not you." But the trouble is that he's acting it out, not telling you about it.

**Harriet:**   I was thinking that the termination is going to be very difficult for him, because you have had a really significant relationship with him and also because of his previous experiences with people leaving. You would need a lot of time to deal with that.

**Ellen:**   I do plan to talk about it.

**Doug:**   He is the one who should be talking about it. Instead of that, he's talking about sex and his mother and all this stuff about how he used to get her to do little favors for him when she was especially busy.

**Gail:** Well, I don't think that's just "stuff." It's very important to him. He was also talking about how his parents made mistakes with him, since he was their first child, and how they did better with his younger brothers.

**Harriet:** I agree with Gail. Wouldn't it throw a lot of light on the scene if, every time he said "mother," you read it as "Ellen"?

**Ellen:** Yes, it would. He is obviously saying these things about me. This time he even came up several times with the phrase "I could control mother." He said, "Most of the time I could control mother and get her to do what I wanted even if she had a million other things to do."

**Gail:** He's surely telling you that you have a million other things to do, so that you are now leaving the agency, and if he could now only control you the way he used to control his mother, he could get you to stay.

**Instructor:** That makes very good sense. He has probably caught on by now that he is, if not your very first client, at least one of your first. And you've made your mistakes on him, as his parents did, so now you should do something for him to make up for it, as his mother did. And if not, he'll take his revenge by getting sicker, coming late, and so on.

**Ellen:** Oh, I missed that totally.

**Allan:** You did say yourself that this termination business is making him anxious, but it hasn't been talked about much.

**Ellen:** No, I guess we both put it off.

**Fran:** Is it making you feel guilty that you are leaving him?

**Ellen:** I guess it is. I am going to recommend another therapist to him, but still—

**Instructor:** He is exerting an enormous pull on you. Naturally enough. You have been very involved with this man. He is one of your first, and you have been seeing him longer than most of the clients we've talked about here.

**Ellen:**   I was feeling some of those things during the sessions, and now I realize that I was trying not to be aware of them. I keep wondering if there might be some way that I could continue to work with him even though I'm no longer at that agency.

**Fran:**   You really have to make up your mind firmly about that before you can talk with him, don't you?

**Ellen:**   Yes, and I know that it doesn't make sense for me to go on seeing him. I really can't do it.

**Instructor:**   But your continuing to think about it indicates how hard the termination is for you as well as for him.

**Ellen:**   It's hard to stop when we're not really finished.

**Gail:**   I'm wondering if you had an ideal situation where you could see him as long as you and he liked, at what point would you feel good about terminating with him?

**Bob:**   I was thinking that too. You have an investment in him and you have goals for him and for yourself, and if you terminated without arriving at those goals you leave yourself hanging as well as him.

**Doug:**   Well, I wonder how long I could work with a person like this, and could you ever be sure when your goals were met?

**Allan:**   It could take another hundred years to resolve all his difficulties.

**Instructor:**   Is that what was behind Gail's question, that you might go on with him forever?

**Gail:**   Yes, I was thinking, Why should they ever stop?

Seminar members are engaged in discussing a topic that is of interest to all of them. They are now looking questioningly at the instructor, since the illusion dies hard that a person in authority knows all the answers.

**Instructor:**   I don't know why they should. What do you think yourselves? If and when you are in therapy, when would *you* stop?

**Doug**:   If you set yourself a goal when you start, then you know when you reach it.

**Harriet**:   But it's not as simple as that.

**Carl**:   Your goals might change while you are in therapy.

**Gail**:   I don't think you would really ever reach your goal unless you set yourself a very limited one, like getting rid of a particular symptom.

**Bob**:   And even then it might come back if you were under stress.

**Ellen**:   Yes, that's what happens with this client.

**Fran**:   Well, I don't see why anyone should stop as long as they are getting something out of it, and as long as they have the time and money to keep on.

**Allan**:   Maybe the therapist would get tired and fed up, seeing the same person for so long.

**Instructor**:   That varies a lot with different therapists. Some do better with short-term cases. Some like to go on for a long time. If you are seeing a schizophrenic patient and treating him psychoanalytically, ten years is not unheard of. But, of course, you can't see very many patients like that. Often practical matters like time and money enter into it, as Fran mentioned. Or someone moves away, either the therapist or the patient. Or one goes on a long vacation and finds it works all right without the therapy. It's usually a matter of diminishing returns rather than a crystal clear stopping place. It's not like being able to say, as in the case of pneumonia, that your chest is now clear and you can go home.

It is interesting to note that, when the problem was thrown back to them, the seminar members themselves brought out important aspects of the question as to when to terminate. The instructor merely added a few things from her own experience.

**Ellen**:   Well, I think that this client has had some very serious problems. When he first came there was a question as to whether he could keep his job. There was also a question as to whether he could keep his girlfriend. Now his job seems quite secure and he and his girl are thinking about getting married. But I believe he could get something out of more therapy.

**Gail:**   So, you'll tell him, then, won't you?

**Ellen:**   Yes, I will. He and I both will have to get used to the idea that he can see someone else. Maybe then this resurgence of his symptoms will calm down.

**Instructor:**   I think it probably will. He's not going to let you go easily, though. It will help if you interpret to him firmly yet sympathetically that you know he has a lot of feelings about your leaving, and some of them may seem childish to him. They are nevertheless natural and understandable. It will be in his interest if he can talk them out, instead of reverting to old patterns and losing the time he still has with you by missing appointments.

Ellen was able to refer the client to another therapist, and the termination did take place without too great difficulty.

Since this case was continued over a longer period of time than was usual in the seminar, it was not surprising that both Ben and Ellen should develop strong feelings toward each other. Without the help of the seminar or some other supervisory assistance, the relationship might have become too much for Ellen to handle. The problem for the seminar was to allow Ellen to become aware of her personal involvement with Ben and to help her to shift it from a personal to a therapeutic relationship. Since she was conscientiously committed to her profession, this was not so difficult. The transformation of the relationship took place by itself as Ellen became aware of her dependency, possessiveness, and wish to give over control of the situation to Ben. As she became clearer about her own side of the relationship, she was able to see what Ben was unwittingly trying to do to her in making her into a mother or a lover who should exist for him alone. Only then was she able to show him what he was doing without either condemnation or approval, so that he could himself become free of the entanglement with her.

# CHAPTER 8

‼‼‼‼‼‼‼‼‼‼‼‼‼‼‼‼‼‼‼‼‼‼‼‼‼‼‼‼‼‼‼‼‼‼‼‼‼‼‼‼‼‼‼‼‼‼‼‼‼

# FAILURES OF
# THE SEMINAR

This chapter includes four presentations in which the seminar failed to bring any new light to the student who was presenting. They are included here because the reader may find it illuminating to understand the reasons for failure. They also illustrate the fact that not every session of the seminar was an exhilarating success. Fortunately, some of the other seminar members learned something in these sessions in spite of the lack of enlightenment experienced by the presenter.

## Section 1
## An Interruption and a Scapegoat

This section is an excerpt that was not part of a scheduled presentation but was essentially an interruption of the usual proceedings. Bob has announced that he has something pressing on his mind that he wants to bring up before the regular case presentation. It becomes clear that the fact of the interruption has so irritated the instructor and some of the seminar members that their interventions are taking the form of covert attacks on Bob. While the content of the comments is sensible, the tone is such that Bob cannot hear it.

The overt issue is the degree of responsibility that a therapist should assume for his client. Investment of the therapist in the client's well-being is an important parameter in effective therapy. But the investment is sometimes more for the sake of the therapist than for the client. Unfortunately, the therapist's need to gratify his own sense of importance to his client could not usefully be pursued in this case because of the affect involved.

**Bob:**    I'd like to bring up a question before we begin today.

**Instructor:**    Okay. Go ahead.

**Bob:**    Six months ago I saw a client and treated him, using behavior therapy. I used desensitization. He had a phobia about speaking before groups. At the end of three months he was doing well, but he terminated because of other obligations that made it difficult for him to keep appointments. When we terminated I told him to contact the agency again if he found he was having any more difficulties. He hasn't done it, and I'm wondering if there is any way I could contact him. If everything is going okay, I'll drop it. Otherwise I'd like to see him for psychodynamic, not behavior, therapy. Is this an appropriate question for the seminar?

**Instructor:**    I don't think the appropriateness for the seminar is the issue.

**Bob:**    I'd like to know what to do.

**Allan:**    Why don't you toss a coin?

**Gail:**    The agency does have a standard follow-up procedure, but I think what you're really asking is permission to pursue this client.

Bob is pressuring the group for a simple yes or no answer. The urgency of his request is experienced as rudeness by some members. Gail is making an attempt to deal with the interruption on a realistic basis so that she can proceed with her own case presentation, which was scheduled for that day.

**Instructor:**    Gail is giving Bob some relevant information about his agency that could settle the question.

**Carl:**    But if you do find through the follow-up that a person is still having problems, would you pursue it?

**Bob:**    That's what I'm asking.

**Instructor:**    I'm wondering, following up on Gail's comment, whether that *is* what you're asking. I don't understand your bringing up the question before you have got the relevant information.

**Bob:**    But I would like to continue with him.

**Allan:**    What if he doesn't ask for help?

**Bob:**    Well, I can't force it on him. I guess I'd like to let him know, if he has problems, that I am still working in the agency and he wouldn't have to repeat his whole story with someone else.

**Doug:**    I'm hearing that you want to protect him. It sounds like you think he's a wishy-washy teenager who can't ask for what he wants. If he perceives that you see him that way, it could be damaging.

**Allan:**    I suppose you don't want to push yourself on him, but maybe that is what you're doing. I'm wondering whether your question was for your client's benefit or your own. I guess some of both is involved, but I'll bet it's not equally divided.

**Carl:**    I acted protectively one time with a client. I don't regret it, but I don't think I was entirely honest with myself. The client told me she had shot up with a dirty needle. I forgot about her mental processes and so on, and I asked her right away about hepatitis symptoms. She didn't want to go to a clinic, but I made her go with me. In other words, I didn't tell her that she was a big girl and she should take care of herself. I made darn sure she got taken care of. I wasn't taking a chance, and it was for my own peace of mind.

**Instructor:**    So, the issue is whether you're going to treat your client like a child who cannot take responsibility for his own life or like a grownup who can. In your case, Carl, you treated your client like a child because she wouldn't take the responsibility for herself. Is that right?

**Carl:**    Yes, she wouldn't go by herself.

**Instructor:**    This is an issue that has to be decided in each individual case. Bob seems to want to treat his client like a child. I wonder what makes you assume he's in trouble.

**Bob:**    I don't know.

**Instructor:**    There are no data; there's no evidence. Right?

**Bob:**    Right, but I'm concerned that he terminated because of the stress of other commitments. It was a behavioral contract, and we weren't dealing with anything but the one symptom. I'm wondering if the stress caused a regression or if he was able to use the behavioral technique I had taught him to deal with it. Part of my curiosity is intellectual.

**Instructor:**    You say you're curious, but the fact that the agency has a follow-up procedure hadn't entered your mind. And even if it didn't have a regular procedure, you could write a letter over the Director's signature asking for follow-up information. But this doesn't seem like what you want to do. It seems you want to get on the phone with him and drag him back.

The instructor is speaking harshly and in an irritated tone of voice. Other seminar members, particularly Ellen and Allan, seem to feel that Bob needs some support.

**Ellen:**  I've felt that way with some people.

**Allan:**  So have I.

**Instructor:**  Yes, as someone said last week, some of us are probably in this business because we like to mother people. That is not the only reason, but it's important to notice when it comes up, because it's often a danger, I think. It's very easy to slip into the role of "Mother knows best and let me take care of you forever." Some people get counterphobic about it, and instead it's "Out with you at the first possible moment." The only safeguard is to be aware of one's own tendencies.

**Bob:**  Well, things were going fine when we stopped. But he was under stress. He was preparing to take the entrance exam for law school.

**Instructor:**  I'm wondering about your assumption that things are going badly with him now. You left it that he could call the agency; why do you assume he wouldn't follow through on this if he wanted to?

**Bob:**  Because it may be admitting defeat.

**Instructor:**  Possibly. I would find it interesting at some time to go into what actually happened between you two during that last session, but I don't think we can do that now.

**Bob:**  He originally came wanting analysis. I explained to him that behavior therapy might be quicker and more effective, and he was sold on the idea quite easily. In the last session I pointed out that he had learned some techniques he could use on his own, but, if he had further trouble, he shouldn't hesitate to call.

**Doug:**  Wait a minute. First, he says he wants analysis, and I wonder what he really wanted. Second, you say that treatment was successful, but then it wasn't successful, and "We'll have to try something else." I don't get it.

**Bob:** My memory is that I told him if he couldn't cope he should come back.

**Instructor:** So you made that perfectly clear to him and to us. I *am* curious about what analysis meant for him and also for you, Bob. Anyway, the means for finding out how he's getting along are available to you. Why don't you use them? And perhaps you could explore for yourself what you are doing in posing this question before you have collected the relevant information. Anyway, it is now time to go ahead with Gail's presentation.

The instructor is suggesting here that Bob has some hidden agenda that he is loathe to bring out. Bob is unable to get at the heart of his concern for his client. He reported later that he feared he had some responsibility for doing more than he had, even though the client did not ask for it. He is also unable to look into his puzzling behavior in omitting to use the follow-up procedures and in interrupting the regular seminar presentation as if he had an emergency on his hands. This is all the more baffling since the instructor was available to individual students for consultation whenever problem situations arose between their presentations.

This excerpt illustrates how difficult and perhaps impossible it is to do any useful work when the irritation of seminar members with each other is not explored, and especially when the instructor participates in it. The irritation in this case had various sources. The most important one lay in an initial mistake on the part of the instructor when she agreed too readily and without investigation that an interruption of the scheduled proceedings of the seminar should take place. When Bob asked to bring up a question before the regular presentation she did not consider the consequences of her casually spoken "Okay. Go ahead." The students shared some measure of responsibility for this, since no one objected to her willingness to allow the interruption.

It is not unusual to find that irritation arises when a mistake has been made and not acknowledged as such. Someone other than the person or persons making the mistake is then found as the scapegoat. Bob plays that role in this section. In fact, he fitted into the role very neatly since he was occupying a scapegoat position in general at that particular time in the life of the group. This role had not been commented on by the instructor or anyone else. It is easy to see in hindsight that the instructor's ready acquiescence to his request had in it some measure of guilt at having allowed him to be treated rather badly by the group on several occasions. During this time he learned very little. In bringing up a problem out of turn, he was expressing the wish for some special and positive attention for himself without asking for it directly from the group, which had treated him badly, just as he wanted to give special and positive attention to his client without being asked for it. He had actually felt guilty that he had treated his client badly in letting him go when he did, but this was largely outside of his awareness. These processes became clear in an individual interview with the instructor later. After that they could become clarified in the group.

### Section 2
### The Stubborn Student

This section is another instance in which the failure of the seminar has to do with indirectly expressed irritation on the part of the instructor and the other seminar members toward the presenter. This time the irritation comes from disapproval of what the presenting student has done with his client. Carl, the presenter, committed himself to a point of view and dug in his heels, so that he was not only unmovable on this point but was unable to hear anything that the other seminar members had to say. It is important to understand the interaction between the stubbornness of his defensive position and the irritation of the instructor and the seminar. They are two sides of a relationship that explain each other. It is not really possible to say which came first. It would be easy to point out that the presenter made a blunder and that the instructor questioned it in such a way that the presenter became defensive. But students often made blunders, and the instructor often questioned a technical move on the part of a presenting student without its resulting in the kind of stalemate that occurs in this section. Subtle factors like the mood of the seminar, the sensitivity of the presenter on that particular day, and the degree of negative criticism and irritation present in the instructor's voice or facial expression all played a role in determining the course taken by the ensuing discussion. To concentrate on one of these factors alone would obscure the importance of the others and would overlook the responsibility of each member of the group for augmenting the failure.

The client in this case was an attractive young woman whose presenting problem was that she was compulsively promiscuous.

**Carl:**   I'm really confused about this client. When she first told me her story I couldn't help thinking how melodramatic it was, and I thought she was putting on an act. She was always getting herself beaten up or mistreated in some terrible way. There were awful scenes and hair-raising escapes. It was like a movie. Not wanting to be presumptuous, I shared this thought with her and asked her if others also might perceive her this way.

**Instructor:**   You would have considered it presumptuous not to say anything at all at that point?

**Carl:**   It would be presumptuous to be sure of my perception, so I shared it with her and asked if it was right instead of saying it *is* right.

**Instructor:**   There are other possibilities besides being absolutely sure you're right and telling the client all your thoughts.

It is not lost upon Carl that the instructor is critical of the way he has proceeded. He becomes defensive at this point and never actually changes his position during the rest of the session.

**Harriet:**   I didn't see that she was putting on an act. Did you think that was really her problem?

**Carl:**   No, her problem is that she lets others dominate her and make all her decisions for her. She knows this, but she says she can't help it. Whenever a guy says he wants to go to bed with her she feels she has to do it, even though she doesn't like herself much afterward. She blames her parents for it. I tried to discourage her from this kind of thinking. I wanted her to substitute another way of thinking, where she can see that she can change herself if she wants to. I tried to show her that she could do that. We identified different ways she was letting other people control her. I encouraged her to explicate the choices she had and to make better choices.

**Ellen:**   How did she respond to that?

**Carl:**   She seemed to like it. For a while she seemed better, too. She said no to a couple of guys and felt good about that. I found her more attractive than I had in the beginning. One day I noticed her perfume, and she had on an especially attractive blouse. I told her I was finding her more attractive than I had in the beginning.

**Instructor:**   What do you think made you tell her that?

The instructor again disapproves, but does not say so directly. Carl, however, surely notices her tone of voice.

**Carl:**   I wanted her to have an authentic relationship. I wanted her to know how I felt about her. It made me feel more comfortable to be honest with her about my feelings.

**Instructor:**   How did she respond?

**Carl:**   I don't remember exactly.

**Instructor:**   You mentioned that you were confused about this client. Can you say more about that?

**Carl:**   I don't understand what has happened. Things went up and now they are down. She seems to have slipped back into her old behavior. For a while she seemed stronger and she could use her strength in her own interest. She was becoming more assertive in her relationships with men. Now it's all slipped away again. She says she knows she should be different, but she can't help herself.

**Ellen:** (Slightly sarcastically.) There seems to be a lot of slip-page!

**Doug:** (Laughing.) I was having sexual fantasies, too!

**Instructor:** I'm sorry to interrupt the enjoyment, but I think we're losing sight of the client and of Carl's problem with her.

**Allan:** I was feeling annoyed with Carl. Maybe I'm envious of him. But I felt that he was thinking about what was good for him and not enough about what was good for the client. I wouldn't have said those things to this client.

**Gail:** I think she got better because she was using you the way she used all the other men. She let you dominate her. You told her what to do and how to think, and she did it.

**Instructor:** That makes sense to me. We don't know, however, what happened next. What do you think, Carl?

**Carl:** I think it was important to the client for me to be honest with her. She has never had an authentic relationship with a man. I wanted to give her one.

**Instructor:** But you said, didn't you, that she is getting worse?

The instructor feels quite disapproving of the way Carl has gone about his work with this client, but thinks that a direct statement of this would not be helpful. She is trying to bring him to a realization that his approach has not resulted in the client's improvement, in the hope that he might then question it. The strategy does not work. It would have been just as well and probably better to proceed more directly.

**Ellen:** I don't think you can give anyone a relationship, authentic or otherwise.

**Carl:** Well, okay, then I wanted to be authentic with her, so that she could learn to be authentic with me.

**Gail:** It's a nice sentiment, but are you going to tell her, every time she is more attractive or less attractive to you personally? What is that supposed to do for her?

**Carl:** I said what it was supposed to do for her. I don't just want to sit expressionless and be a blank screen for her. I don't approve of that.

**Instructor:** In avoiding a caricature of the traditional psychoanalyst, one may go to the other extreme of saying whatever comes to one's mind to a client. I think the word *authentic* has become a sort of slogan now for justifying stepping out of the role of therapist. If the client is coming to you as an expert, she is not coming to you as to a friend or a peer. You have a task to do and a role to respect, just as you respect her role as client. I am not advocating dishonesty, but I do not think it is in the client's interest to forget that your role is not her role. In this particular case, I think you can see the results of giving up your role.

The instructor is making an important point, but the mood of the seminar is such that the lesson cannot be learned, at least not by Carl.

**Carl:** You mean you think that's why she got worse?

**Instructor:** Yes, and, as Gail said, probably also why she initially got better. But none of this was understood or even talked about. So it's not surprising that she acts out. Allan had a client something like this. Could it help if you told about her?

**Allan:** She was just a *little* bit like this woman. I found her at first homely and lifeless and later much more attractive to me personally, but I didn't tell her that. I do remember telling her that I thought she wanted me to find her attractive. But that was talking about her, not about me.

**Carl:** I didn't want to just talk about her. I wanted to tell her how *I* felt.

The instructor has only compounded the trouble by essentially making a comparison between Carl and Allan, of whose work she had approved. Carl is simply becoming more stubborn, and there is no movement toward deeper understanding.

**Allan:**   Sometimes you can help a client by telling him what you think. It depends on what the client makes of it.

Allan is obviously somewhat embarrassed at having been set up as the "good therapist" against Carl as the "bad therapist," and he tries to mediate.

**Ellen:**   Yes, I think that's right. This woman made a bad thing of it. First she wanted to do what you said. And then she must have been disappointed in you, since you didn't carry through and take her to bed. So she goes back to her old patterns.

**Bob:**   Has she said how she feels about you?

**Carl:**   I don't exactly remember. It would be good if she could get really angry at me.

**Instructor:**   I was just thinking of the fury of a woman scorned. She is taking a much more effective revenge on you than by getting angry. I have to confess that when people talk about being authentic I always wonder what they are hiding. You are not usually so ponderous, Carl. Does the way this woman throws herself at men bother you? It might well, I should think.

The instructor has tried to rescue the situation and may have partly succeeded, but it is too late to do much more in this session.

**Carl:**   Maybe. I do feel confused, and there are things I don't remember clearly. I never had a client like this before.

**Allan:**   I think she would be very hard to work with.

Allan is trying to reconcile again.

**Harriet:**   I thought you strongly disapproved of what you called her melodrama, but you didn't tell her that.

**Instructor:**   Just as we didn't tell Carl that we disapproved of his way of handling her. Or perhaps I should say *I* disapproved.

**Ellen:**   It made me feel very uncomfortable. I felt something was hiding, too. It was as if you were protesting too much about being honest with her.

Carl:   But I did want to be honest with her.

Carl cannot get beyond this during this session. It is too difficult for him to see that he is using what he calls authenticity as a defense to keep himself from seeing his deep disapproval of this client's behavior. He has tried to sermonize her into better ways and has tried to reward her improvement, but he has failed to see that she is expecting much more of him and that she is almost bound to get worse in an effort to get him to do more for her.

In the introduction to this section, a number of factors were enumerated that played a role in the failure of the session. One of them, probably the most important, is worth elaborating. The stand that Carl took in representing "authenticity" set off strong reactions of irritation in the instructor and in some other seminar members. In retrospect, it is possible to see that quite a bit of anxiety was involved that did not surface clearly during the session. The troublesome thought nagging at the back of the instructor's mind, though not well formulated at the time, was, What an impossible bind one puts a beginning therapist in by encouraging him to be forthright, to call a spade a spade, and not to collude with his client's self-deception, and then jumping down his throat when he thinks he is doing just that!

Or, to put it another way: Who is to judge, when a person claims that he is being authentic, whether he really is or not? The instructor knows very well that she cannot simply assert that her judgment is correct in this. She is quite convinced that Carl is deceiving himself and that he has been seduced by this young woman into self-serving flattery of her when he tells her he finds her more attractive than he had before. She also knows that accusing a person of self-deception is not conducive to greater honesty. This quandary, which is not easy to resolve even when it is clearly seen, led to the instructor's sarcasm in her first intervention and to the unhelpful disapproval evident in her later comments. The other seminar members are affected in a similar way but to varying degrees. On other occasions, in similar situations, fellow students have been more effective than the instructor in opening the eyes of one of their peers to what he was up to.

## Section 3
## A Very Wealthy Client

The failure in this case stemmed from a particular anxiety on the part of the student therapist that could not be opened up in the seminar. It is possible, however, that if the instructor and the other seminar members had been more sensitive to the problem earlier in the session, a way might have been found to melt the frozen defenses of Fran, who was presenting.

The client in this section is a very wealthy, good-looking young woman from a prominent family who came into therapy at the recommendation of her internist. She had complained to her physician about a number of symptoms that had been identified as functional, including mild headaches and occasional outbreaks of dermatitis. Fran has told about her client's history, which seemed to be relatively uneventful in childhood but included an unusual number of moves from one school to another during adolescence. The client is at present attending a junior college. Fran adds as an afterthought to her description of the client that she dresses extremely simply.

**Fran:** So what am I supposed to do about her headaches? Of course, she does not notice anything about when they occur. On the dermatitis she is a bit more specific. Whenever she has a specially important party to go to, she has a breaking out on her face. If she goes to the Caribbean on a winter vacation and wants to wear a beautiful bathing suit, she breaks out on her legs and arms.

Fran has spoken in a rather cold, sarcastic tone of voice. Allan in his next statement seems to be reacting to her harshness with a kind of elder-brotherly sympathy for the client.

**Allan:** Well, that *is* tough on a kid. Things like that are naturally important to her.

**Fran:** I suppose it is tough, but what should I do about it? I wish her internist had given her some salve to put on her skin. *I* don't know how to fix her dermatitis.

**Instructor:** You surely have attempted to get clear with her what it is that you can do and what you can't.

**Fran:** I've tried, but she is not very cooperative. She came because somebody sent her, and she probably doesn't see much point in it.

**Instructor:** Have you established with her what kind of problem you can and will work on together?

**Fran:** She wants to get rid of her symptoms.

**Gail:** But you can't go directly at them, especially if she doesn't know what situations they occur in.

**Fran:** No, I guess not.

Fran is exhibiting an extraordinary lack of curiosity and an unwillingness to examine the trouble she presents. Her obtuseness and stubbornness leave the seminar members at a loss for a solution, since it is not Fran's usual behavior. In his next statement Carl tries to open the discussion with a challenge.

**Carl:** You make her sound kind of hopeless, but I'm not sure she really is.

**Ellen:** Why did she go to so many different schools?

Ellen has finally broken through the preoccupation with somatic symptoms to try to look into another aspect of the client's behavior that might bear some psychological investigation.

**Fran:** When she was about fifteen her family was living abroad, and first she moved from a local private school to a very fancy school in Switzerland. She didn't like that because the classes were dull, so then she went to a very well-known girls' school in Massachusetts with high academic standards. After that she wanted to be closer to her family who had by then moved back to the United States, so she went to a public school near Philadelphia. She didn't like that either, but by that time she had almost finished high school and she thought she would try the junior college she is in now.

**Ellen:** There must be something about that history that would bear looking into. Does she like the school she's at now?

**Fran:** Not much, but I don't blame her for that. They're a bunch of girls from rich families who don't think about anything except their dates and their clothes. Most of them don't have a brain in their heads.

**Bob:** Does she?

**Fran:** I think she probably does.

Fran sounds as if she were reluctant to admit that the client has any positive attribute.

**Allan:** Well, that's a help.

**Fran:** In fact she has just about everything that anyone could want.

**Instructor:** Perhaps that's the trouble.

**Fran:** You mean she has too much?

**Instructor:** No, I really meant perhaps that's the trouble between you and her.

The instructor has moved in too rapidly here. Although the trouble in the relationship seems obvious to her, it is not so to Fran, who wants to maintain that it is all in the client. The instructor missed a chance to pick up on Fran's view of the client as having "too much."

**Fran:** I don't think I really understand what you mean.

**Instructor:** Well, skip it. Maybe it's not the time to go into it now.

**Gail:** If she moved around to all those different schools, she may not have any close friends. Did she complain about that?

**Fran:** Yes, a bit, in a defensive sort of way. She seemed to feel criticized when I asked her about friends, both male and female. She said she gets along all right with people, and I couldn't extract much information from her. But she does not have any close friends here, and she is rather vague about any from the other schools she went to.

**Gail:** She sounds as if she might be terribly lonely. Could you work with her on that?

**Fran:** If she's interested I could, but I don't really know if she is.

**Carl:** You don't sound as if *you* were very interested.

**Fran:** I just don't know how to get beyond the symptoms. I'd really like to send her to a psychiatrist who could prescribe something for her. She can certainly afford it. It is just convenient for her to come to see me. She doesn't even have to walk across the street. If she went to a psychiatrist it would take an effort.

**Instructor:** It is really a handicap for this girl that she is so rich, isn't it?

The instructor has now backtracked and is putting the problem on the client. But she has phrased it in a slightly sarcastic way that Fran cannot accept.

**Fran:** Well, not exactly.

**Bob:** I don't understand why you don't like this girl. She's bright and good-looking. She isn't attacking you or threatening suicide or doing anything unpleasant.

**Fran:** I don't dislike her. I just don't know how to deal with her symptoms.

**Gail:** But Fran, you don't have to deal with her symptoms. She sounds like a very reserved person who can't tell a stranger that she is miserable and lonely. You aren't hearing her.

**Instructor:** I think we should respect Fran's wish to send this girl to someone else. Probably we should do that more often when we feel that we cannot work with a client. There is as much risk in denying our professional limitations as there is in misrepresenting ourselves to our clients. But in the interest of learning, could we try to look into what makes her difficult to work with?

The instructor has come to the conclusion that it is best to remove some pressure from Fran. She also hopes to facilitate Fran's thinking about her relationship with this client by opening up the way for her to get out of it, but the strategy does not work.

**Fran:** I just don't see how I can work with these physical symptoms when she doesn't see any connection with anything.

**Allan:** But Fran, she *does*. She said she gets the dermatitis whenever there is an occasion when she supposedly would like to look especially nice.

**Gail:** You're not usually so unsympathetic or unempathic with clients, Fran. It really seems as if you don't like this girl. Isn't that true?

**Fran:** No, there isn't anything wrong with her.

**Instructor:** Do you feel that you could manage better if there *were* something wrong with her? Her ailments don't seem very serious, do they?

**Fran:** Well, no, they don't. I've had much worse.

In her last remark Fran betrays that she is very preoccupied with a comparison of herself to the client. If she could bring this into focus it would be helpful to her and to the work of therapy. But she cannot get to it at this time and place.

**Instructor:** And you didn't have an internist and a psychotherapist to go to either. Is that right?

**Fran:** Oh, but I had friends to talk to.

The instructor has again moved too quickly. Fran is obviously very sensitive in the matter of comparing herself to the client and she is warning the seminar members that they are approaching too close. The instructor decides to heed the warning. She subsides for a while and waits to see what the others can do.

**Gail:** Well, maybe *she* doesn't have friends to talk to. I think that must be one of her problems.

**Carl:** Why don't you try working with her on the business of making friends?

**Allan:** I can't get it out of my head that this girl's wealth and her prominent family are playing a role in this.

**Ellen:** I think Allan is right. Maybe you could find out what it means to her to come from the kind of family she comes from. Even though she's been in some fancy schools, she's also been in a public school and she's lived in the world too. She knows that not everyone is driven to school by a chauffeur.

**Fran:** I think she'd wonder what that had to do with her headaches and dermatitis.

**Allan:** Maybe it has plenty.

Fran has a real problem in that her client is apparently interested primarily in the relief of minor physical symptoms for which no medical treatment was prescribed. The internist prescribed a psychological procedure instead, but the client has evinced little interest in this so far. The seminar members suspect that Fran has not given her client sufficient opportunity or invitation to become interested in what might be her psychological problems. They also suspect that Fran has psychological reasons of her own for helping the client to maintain her lack of interest in anything but her physical symptoms. As long as Fran limits herself to curing the headache and dermatitis directly, she is stymied and will have no recourse but to let the client go. This is clearly what she wants to do. The other students want to get to the bottom of the problem between therapist and client, but Fran has quite stubbornly dug in her heels. The result is a stalemate. Harriet has been looking thoughtful but has said nothing up to this point. Now she leans forward and speaks in a very serious manner directly to Fran.

**Harriet:** Fran, I was brought up in a very poor neighborhood, and sometimes my mother wondered if she'd have enough money at the end of the month to buy groceries for us. She was born in Europe and she still speaks English with an accent. I think if I were in your place, I would be very uncomfortable with this girl, who sounds like her ancestors came over on the Mayflower and have been running the country ever since. I think I would envy her and I would think thoughts like, Why should I be bothering about her little bit of dermatitis when people are out of jobs and hungry and worried about how they're going to pay the rent? I would resent having to be nice and kind and helpful to her. Maybe you don't have thoughts like that, but I do. It's hard for most of us now, as students, to make ends meet. And she's never had to think about anything like that.

(The seminar members look at Harriet appreciatively and nod in agreement.)

**Gail:** I think Harriet has made a very straight and clear statement, and I go along with her.

**Bob:** I do too.

**Fran:** I hear what you say and maybe you're right, Harriet. But I'm just not aware of feeling like that. My client doesn't in any way rub it in that she comes from a prominent family, and when I'm with her I've been able to forget it. I think I told you her clothes are so simple you would never know she has a fortune.

**Ellen:** But why do you want to forget it? It's probably important to her even if, as you claim, it's not to you.

**Fran:** Does it have to be important? Why does it matter which side of the tracks people are brought up on?

Fran is now showing signs of a great deal of tension and distress. She knows very well that the experiences people have early in life tend to shape their attitudes and behavior. But she has been, so to speak, cornered in a place that is painful, and she cannot do anything with it at this time. The group has not been unusually rough with her. In fact, Harriet spoke in a very moving way and with a great deal of empathy for Fran's situation. But there are times when an individual cannot respond to any more group pressure.

**Instructor:**  I'd just like to repeat what I said about respecting Fran's wish to turn this client over to someone else. I think her inclination is right. When we feel unable to work with a client who needs further therapy, it becomes a professional and an ethical responsibility to refer the client to a more suitable person. It might be that a physician could find some way to alleviate her symptoms while he is looking at the psychological factors. And even if he didn't, the fact that he is a physician may reassure her that he will take her symptoms seriously. Why don't you make a referral, Fran? And let's stop for today.

This section is an example of a therapist-client relationship that is unfeasible. Although it might be possible to help Fran in individual supervision to work with this client, it is a sufficiently difficult problem to warrant giving up and transferring to someone else. It is apparent to the instructor, to Harriet, and probably to other seminar members that Fran simply cannot accept the envy and resentment that this client brings up in her. If she were to be honest with herself, she would say something like what Harriet has suggested to her, but she has not yet come to terms with her early history sufficiently to be able to do this. Because it does not seem like such a bad thing to the other seminar members to envy more fortunate people, they are a bit insensitive to the fact that in this situation it is apparently unbearable to Fran. Thus they failed in helping her to become aware of the true reasons why she wants to get rid of this client. She does not see that what she wants to get rid of are some unacceptable tendencies in herself.

## Section 4
## The Client Who is Forced Into Therapy

The failure in this session can be ascribed to the intrin-
sically difficult situation that the therapist faced both in the
outer world and in his own inner world. A client who is not
self-referred but is forced or cajoled by some other person to
come into therapy is a common problem in community service
agencies and educational institutions. A student therapist who
has not resolved his own problems with authority is seriously
handicapped in dealing with such a client.

Allan is presenting the case of a fourteen-year-old high
school student whom he has been seeing at the request of the
vice-principal in a school in which he works. The student, Jim,
is said to lack motivation for school achievement. He is absent a
great deal. When he arrives at school, he cuts classes. When he
does go to his classes, he disrupts them so successfully that his
teachers are inclined to encourage his absences, although they
do not admit this. Various teachers have tried to interest him in
some aspect of school work and every one has failed. Allan has
presented what he knows of the boy's history and family background—a broken home, a bitter mother and an alcoholic
father, many upheavals and moves from one place to another—
and is now talking about his once-a-week meetings with Jim.

**Allan:** He comes to our sessions not because they are useful to
him but because they are less boring than his classes. He's very
difficult to talk with, and he's not cooperative at all. When I ask
him questions, his answers are either bland and agreeable—what
he thinks I want to hear—or "I don't know."

There is another problem, too. We meet in a little room
off the vice-principal's office. She doesn't come in, but our sessions are often interrupted by a secretary or one of the adminis-
trative staff coming in to use the files that are in that office.
They say they have to do that.

Jim sees our sessions more or less as a joke. I asked him
what he thought we were doing together, and he said we were
here so that I could get my degree. Someone had told him I was

working toward my doctorate. He's not dumb; he's pretty smart. I told him that whether I saw him or not had no bearing on my degree, but I don't think he bought that, because I asked him again what he thought he was getting out of our meetings and he said, "Well, it's experience for you."

**Instructor:** That's magnanimous of him. But I must say he has a point, and I'm not sure your statement to him was entirely honest. It's true that you'll get your degree whether you see this particular youngster or not. But the work you are doing *is* in connection with your training and with getting your degree. I'm not wanting to quibble, but, as you said, he didn't buy it, and I think it would have been better to say, "Sure, it's experience for me, but that doesn't stop it from being experience for you, too." You'd be on a better footing with him.

**Allan:** Yes, well, I didn't want to get mad at him because it wouldn't have helped. I tried to take it as his expressing some interest in me, and I tried to explain that I was there for him and not because it had something to do with my degree and that I could perform a function for him and with him. But I don't think he was hearing me, because he said he was going to stick it out in school for two more years because he has to, and then he'll quit and get a job.

Allan's statement that he didn't want to get mad is, of course, a giveaway that he *is* mad at the boy. That is very understandable, since he is frustrated by him at every turn. Allan also has reason to be angry at the school authorities, but he is trying very hard to push both of these feelings out of his mind while he concentrates like a "good therapist" on the welfare of his client, or at least on his conception of the welfare of his client.

**Instructor:** Do you know whether he is aware of any other trouble in his life aside from his conflict with the school authorities?

**Allan:** I asked him several times and he either says everything is okay or "I don't know."

**Fran:** When you were talking about why you were seeing him, I was wondering what you said exactly. I don't think he understands.

**Allan:** His comments showed that he didn't understand, so I explained again who I was, how I had gotten there and what my purpose was for being there. I explained to him that I had an interest in working with students like him.

**Fran:** What kind of students?

**Allan:** High school students in trouble. I told him I knew he wasn't attending classes, and I was there to try to get some idea as to what he feels about his classes and why he chooses not to go. And I asked him if he realized that it won't be to his advantage if he quits before graduating, because he might need a diploma to get a job.

**Bob:** What did he say?

**Allan:** Nothing, except that school is boring. He says he doesn't know why, it just is.

**Gail:** If I were in his place, I might feel you were just trying to get me to go to class like everyone else. It sounds as if it's been structured as a battle between him and school, and you are another enemy on the side of the school.

**Allan:** I was thinking about how he was selected for counseling.

This statement of Allan's seems to change the subject from Gail's comment about the battle between the client and the school, but it can be interpreted as an unwitting reference to Allan's own battle with the school of which he is not sufficiently aware.

**Instructor:** I think he was selected because he is the most troublesome kid to the vice-principal, but obviously he is not the most gratifying candidate for individual psychotherapy. I believe the chief counselor at that school would have found you a better client, but he was trying to be tactful to the new vice-principal and so he left the selection to her. All of this is not very helpful to you, except that it teaches you something about working in institutions.

**Allan:**   Maybe it was set up to fail.

Allan is beginning to think about how the cards are stacked against him, but he is not yet seeing how he has contributed to the situation.

**Instructor:**   I remember when you first met him; it was in the vice-principal's office. One of his teachers was there and said to Jim, "How are you ever going to get an education if you don't come to class?" Since you were there and didn't object to the statement, he's probably got you pegged as having the same attitude, and you have played into it a little bit. Also, the place where you see him links you to the vice-principal and the whole school administration.

**Allan:**   I've tried to avoid implying that he had to go to his classes, but I'm trying to find out why he doesn't want to go.

Allan is misapplying the formula of traditional psychotherapy with responsible adults, in which both patient and therapist are presumably interested in finding out the reasons for behavior.

**Carl:**   Have you found out?

**Allan:**   Well, no. When I asked him how he thought we could make the sessions more meaningful and useful, his answer was to make them shorter.

**Harriet:**   He gives me the impression that no matter what you did, he'd win.

**Gail:**   He'd outsmart you.

**Allan:**   Right. Everything he says beyond "I don't know" is a smart answer. I pointed that out to him and, if it made a dent, it was so slight as not to be noticeable. He just came back with another smart comment. I didn't play into it, but I think he wanted to agitate me.

**Instructor:**   If you think he is saying something to agitate you, could you comment to the effect that other people have probably been treating him the way he is now treating you?

**Allan:**   I haven't really tried that, but I don't know that I would get anything from him. I'd like to find out why he's staying away from school and what he does when he's not there.

**Fran:**   From his point of view it's silly to talk about school. I'm sure he thinks it's absurd.

**Allan:**   But he said he wanted to work after he gets out of school. I tried to get him to see how school would fit in for him if he was going to get a job, how he could get a better job if he had gone to school.

**Instructor:**   Well, you see, you are firmly fixed as a person on the side of the school in this battle that has been drawn up.

**Fran:**   What if you took the line that you don't give a damn whether he goes to school or not?

**Allan:**   I can't change all of a sudden. I try to present myself as someone who is concerned to make things better for him as an individual apart from the school administration or his parents or his gang or anyone else. That was the approach I tried, but I don't seem to get anywhere with it.

Allan is trying hard and conscientiously to do something for this boy, but he has not sufficiently considered the preoccupations that the client has brought to the sessions or the factors that are operating in the environment. He is still trying to fit Jim into the model of therapy that he is used to with older clients, who seek out a therapist and are expecting to work psychologically.

**Doug:**   When you say you want to make things better for him, you are thinking about what would make things better for you. You believe it is good to go to school, and we were all raised to believe that. But he doesn't buy it. I get the impression that you believe all his problems would be solved if he would just go to school.

**Allan:**   I wouldn't go that far.

**Doug:**   What I'm saying is that in your value system, school is good. He must sense that you are trying to get him to think the same way you do, and he is going to fight it. You are trying to impose your values on him.

Doug is bringing out the important point that therapists can work easily with clients whose goals and values they share. The problem then is to discover why the clients are not achieving their goals or living according to the values they cherish. But when the values are unknown, unformed, or significantly different, the problem is more complex and more difficult. Allan is not admitting that this is part of his problem. The seminar has now added its own pressures to those under which he was already struggling. He is weighed down by the client, the school, and his own inner conflicts. He is unable to do anything but fall back upon his previously stated position.

**Allan:**   No, I'm not trying to impose on him. I'm trying to present myself to him as an individual wanting to help. I just tried to get him to accept me as an individual.

**Instructor:**   I think it's a mistake to try to get a kid like this to accept you by being nice to him. The other counselors and teachers have tried that ad nauseam, and he sees through it or refuses to have anything to do with it. I think you have to go the other way round with him and be pretty tough, which can also be deeply kind. He can't imagine that anybody does anything except for his own interest. So you could say, "Sure, I'm out to get something. I want to get my doctorate. And what do you want to get? Is what I want necessarily against what you want?" Maybe you could get him to see that he has immediately set you up as an enemy. It would take some doing to get him to imagine that you are not. You would have to prove that to him, and it's a tough job. You might as well keep on trying, since you really might get something out of it for yourself and it's unlikely that you'll do him any harm.

**Ellen:**   Allan is a very empathic person, and his just being with this boy might be a good thing for Jim.

**Gail:** What would be the harm in playing some games with him in the sessions, cards or checkers or something?

**Carl:** Kids show all kinds of behavior that you can talk about when they play games, cheating and being afraid to win or lose and all kinds of things.

**Fran:** I think that's what I would do, too.

**Instructor:** If you go on as you are right now, you may become so frustrated that you would do something destructive to him. I think you do need to get out of the rut you are in.

**Allan:** I might try playing a game with him.

The seminar has come up with a practical suggestion that turned out to be quite useful to Allan, at least in keeping the sessions bearable until the end of the school year. The suggestion arose at a time when the seminar members were becoming aware of the impossible situation that Allan was in. The comments and suggestions up to that point had not been helpful, and Allan was unable to see the internal conflict in which he was involved. Like most young people who are in training to become professionals, he is not without sympathy for the rebellious dropout from school, since he has suffered under the system quite a bit himself. On the other hand, he has made the decision to buy into the system and get his doctorate. Soon *he* will be in a position of authority in a school or university, a hospital or clinic. Allan is dependent on the university to award him his degree. He is dependent on the school in which he is working to provide field experience and a recommendation. But he is highly critical of both. Whether it is a school or a clinic or hospital, the flaws and stupidities of administration always provide excellent rationalizations for complaints against management. Allan is quite typical of the young professional in his deeply ambivalent attitude toward authority, especially in the educational system. He is allied to authority through his identification with parents and teachers. He is fighting against the system as a young rebel who wants to overthrow or at least to reform it. In this particular instance, Allan was leaning in the direction of identification with authority. At the same time he could not deny that the school had put him, with his permission, in a practically impossible situation. If he gave up or did not get the student to attend his classes, it was a black mark for him as a counselor. If he allied himself strongly with the school's attitude toward Jim, he felt that he was letting down his client. All of these pulls and tugs were too much to become aware of at that time. It is not surprising that the seminar failed to find a way to be of much help in this situation.

CHAPTER 9

```
╔══════════════════════════════════════════════════════════╗
```

# A NEAR FAILURE
# THAT TURNED
# INTO A SUCCESS

This seminar could easily have become a failure. It took quite a bit of time and work before the therapist presenting his case could let down his defenses enough to allow himself to learn something. Initially the group made it difficult for him. This excerpt illustrates what can happen when a therapist is displeased and actually somewhat ashamed of what he has been doing with a client, but cannot look into the reason for his bumbling.

172

Doug is presenting a young woman recently separated from her husband. Both before her marriage and after the separation she had formed a number of brief liaisons with men that had all ended when she became dissatisfied with each partner in turn. At the time of this interview she was working as a saleswoman, a job far below her capacity. After sketching her history and telling something about the course of the earlier sessions, Doug puts a question to the seminar. His tone of voice might have warned the seminar members that it would not be simple for him to hear an answer. His tone is harsh, strained, and a bit quavering as he conforms to the instructor's request that, if possible, presentations be accompanied by a question about the case. The words are exactly right, but the music is false.

**Doug:** I would like to ask the seminar what I am doing to collude with her sick patterns in relating to men and to her former therapists. She really complicates things through obstacles.

**Instructor:** She what?

The instructor has actually heard the words but is responding to her own need to get some clarification in what has seemed to her to be a very obscure presentation, replete with wordy intellectualizations.

**Doug:** She complicates, makes barriers, makes it difficult for someone to work with her, to have a relationship with her, so that you get to the point where you just might want to say, "Oh, good riddance." I want to know what I'm doing that contributes to the pattern.

Again Doug gives lip service to his duty to ask a question, but, as will soon become apparent, he does not allow himself to collaborate in finding an answer.

**Instructor:** You mentioned in your presentation something about a contract. I didn't quite understand what you were referring to.

**Doug:** I drew up a contract with her stating what she would do and stating what I would do, and she said it made sense.

Basically, the contract said that we would cooperate in the sessions in giving serious consideration to her problems and patterns of behavior, and if this did not happen it would be grounds for discontinuing. The contract specified therapist's tasks and client's tasks. She is to attend sessions regularly and on time, cooperate with the therapist, and seriously consider suggestions relative to the changes she wants to make. She is to note, in writing, important insights or points made in the sessions by both client and therapist and develop implications from these points. I explained all this, and we discussed what it meant and the possible steps that could be taken to modify her behavior.

Well, now she is not cooperating. When we get to a problem, she says, "Oh, that's too complicated. I don't have anything more to say."

What I want to know is what should I do now. If I stick to the terms of the contract, I should really break off. But then that probably means goodbye, and I don't like that.

**Carl:** I don't understand what you mean by cooperating and not cooperating.

**Doug:** Well, last session she was discussing her parents and I was asking her about certain aspects of that relationship, and after a while she said, "That's too complicated. I can't say any more." And I felt she could have damn well said some more, but it was making her uncomfortable, and she just wouldn't cooperate with the kind of investigation we were having.

**Harriet:** It sounds to me as if the contract meant it's okay if you are a model client and never put up any resistances, but if you resist, that's not allowed.

**Ellen:** Defenses are not allowed, either.

**Instructor:** When did all this happen with the contract? I am quite confused as to when and how it happened. Did she read something you had written and sign it?

**Doug:** Oh, yes.

**Instructor:**    You actually got her signature on a piece of paper?

**Doug:**    No, she didn't actually sign it. We discussed what it meant, and she said it was agreeable to her.

Confusion in the seminar is apparent. The other students and the instructor are each off on a track of his or her own, supposedly trying to clarify but actually adding to Doug's problems. It was easy to hear in the voice of each person disapproval of the use of a written contract in this way, but the disapproval has not yet been stated directly. Confusion seems to take the place of disapproval. This continues for some time and makes it difficult for Doug to use any of the "helpful," interpretive statements that are offered to him.

**Instructor:**    So she has this piece of paper at home. When did this happen?

**Doug:**    The session before last. It was kind of a wild session. She was just going all over the place. She has every nervous habit you can think of, biting her fingernails, pulling on her hair; she also has a facial tic. And she is a fantastic intellectualizer. I tried to bring her back to the point, but it just got so complicated. I wasn't doing a very good job of holding her to the point.

**Allan:**    I think this raises a question about the efficacy of structuring through something so formal. I think when I try to set up some formalized rules, I get trapped.

**Doug:**    Yeah, the contract may well reflect some fears that I have about failing. The contract may have made it predictable that it was going to fail. I also asked her to give me an autobiographical sketch, and what she gave me was a very interesting journal that she kept a couple of years ago when she was in analysis.

**Instructor:**    She was in psychoanalysis?

**Doug:**    Right. She did that for a while, too. She also saw a gestalt therapist and a counseling psychologist in high school when she was having trouble with her parents. She doesn't quite remember what went on. And after graduation she also saw a psychiatrist. She doesn't remember who initiated that, or what the circumstances were. After she was married, she also saw some kind of a shrink to help her decide whether to leave her husband. During that time she began having very sleepless nights, and the shrink asked her to seriously consider being hospitalized for a while; she went along with the idea until the day before she was to go, and then she called the hospital and said, "No, thank you."

. None of the therapy seems to have worked very well. The problem she brought first to me was: "I want to feel something. I'm not in touch with my feelings." She is very psychologically minded. She only went partway through college, but she has a very impressive repertoire. She makes fine verbal distinctions. You can tell she's been to an analyst's office. She has all the insights, but it is exceedingly difficult for her to change. One thing she has noticed. After she wins someone's affection, she turns off and acts kind of like a castrating bitch. The last session she brought in some of these things, some of these insights.

**Instructor:**   On paper?

**Doug:**   Yes, on paper. I didn't quite like that. I was concerned that the mechanics could ruin the entire thing.

**Bob:**   But didn't you ask her to do that?

**Doug:**   Yes, I did, but at the same time—

**Carl:**   It's a neat distancing device. Such a neat way to keep her away from you or you away from her.

**Doug:**   Yeah, I felt I needed to structure, I needed some way to define something clearly, because she was just running all over the place. I've never done this with a formalized contract before and maybe it was a mistake, but I felt I really needed it to get her to focus on something.

**Instructor:**   I think it was a mistake to think you could legislate it.

Doug's rigidly formal use of a written contract has now been called a mistake, by him as well as by the seminar. The seminar members continue to belabor it in an antagonistic, critical way. They need to have something specific to relate to, in the morass of material presented. As is apparent from the next statement, the comments have not been helpful to Doug.

**Doug:**  I think no matter what I would have done, she would have said, "Yes, I like that," and then she would have resisted it. The last session I felt really terrible, like I didn't do something I should have or I did something I shouldn't have. I felt both of those things, and yet I don't know what I could have done. I felt crippled.

**Allan:**  I think you could have raised the question of your and her responsibility without setting conditions. If you set conditions that won't hold, you are trapped.

**Doug:**  Well, I did feel kind of trapped. I kept thinking that she's not really cooperating, that she's doing her best to resist in a way I can't get at. And then I have another kind of feeling, too, and another kind of investment in this girl. She grew up in the same town that I did. I know where she lived and the grade school she went to and we could have met sometime, though we actually didn't. It just struck me as being kind of a really rotten shame for this girl to get stuck the way she is. In reading her journal I see a very bright gal who has a fantastic battle with herself. She flirts with suicide and gets into all these vicious circles with people. I tried to show her how she was using complexity, like thinking up a billion different angles of something and never doing anything positive for herself. She keeps herself a little girl, never coming to a conclusion, though she really is so intelligent.

**Harriet:**  Doesn't that get you to make the decisions for her if she presents all the complexities and leaves it at that? Do you feel she is saying that you're going to have to help her decide?

Because other issues seemed to be of greater interest to the seminar, the opportunity was missed to point out to Doug that his identification with the client might well be standing in the way of his taking a more consistent therapeutic position with her. Not only do they both come from the same town but they are both very intelligent and are both in the habit of using complex intellectual formulations as defenses to keep from experiencing anxiety.

**Doug:**   In the beginning she did ask me to help her and to tell her what I thought, but the last few times I've decided to throw it back on her.

**Allan:**   When she's trying to be a little girl, that makes you the adult; so you're going to take all the complexities and clear them up for her.

**Instructor:**   I have the impression that we're trying to discuss this with too little information. Could you tell us a little bit about the content of the last session? What were some of the things she talked about?

The instructor has become aware that the seminar is not being useful to Doug, and she tries unsuccessfully to move toward a fresh start.

**Doug:**   At this point it's a little vague. It's going to take a few sessions to define what she really wants to work on, because I don't know what "I'm not in touch with my feelings" means. One of the patterns I mentioned was that she was getting involved with people and then losing interest. She was sexually involved and then turned off sexually.

**Bob:**   Does she talk in those terms? When she comes in, does she talk about complexity or does she give you a "for instance," a concrete example in which this happens?

**Doug:**   She's very psychologically minded.

Doug has not noticed the repetitive quality of his statements. He is quite unable at this point to make a fresh start.

**Bob:**   It's very hard to get any feel for her in talking about the abstract, and I was wondering if this is how she presents it to you—in these abstract terms.

**Doug:**    She does both and maybe I'm confused about focusing, too.

**Bob:**    Could we have a couple of the "for instances"?

**Doug:**    Well, in the last session she mentioned she had visited her parents. Her mother she describes as very cold, unaffectionate, and puritanical. Her father is somewhat warmer, but she is afraid of what he is up to. He sends her presents of underwear, very pretty, feminine things, and writes that he wishes he could see her in them. She is in touch with the sexual nature of what he is doing and she sees it like a triangle. She and Dad against Mom. But her parents give her all kinds of double messages. Sometimes they treat her with contempt, but sometimes even her mother is really nice. On the last visit her mother actually put her arms around her. At that point I was trying to focus on some of the inconsistencies and trying to get a picture, and she comes out with, "Stop, it's too complicated. I don't want to talk about it." And I said, "It's going to be very difficult for us to get anywhere if, because it's complicated, you just throw up your hands."

**Carl:**    Where is it you want to get?

This was rather sharply spoken by Carl. The tone is symptomatic of the mood of the seminar, which is unusually antagonistic. It is, therefore, not surprising that Doug cannot take anything in. The group's disapproval of the written contract was not clearly enough brought out and worked through. Doug could have recognized that the contract was an error if the seminar members had been more direct in their statements, and he might then have proceeded more readily to look at what led him to use it. This is a typical pitfall into which the seminar sometimes fell.

**Doug:**    The first thing is to define some problem areas. Everything she does is so kind of complicated and she just leaves it at that.

**Allan:**    Yeah, but you're just leaving it at that, too.

**Doug:**  Well, I'm trying to break into it.

**Allan:**  But it's not only she; it's also you, who are saying that if it gets too complicated, then we can't work.

**Doug:**  Yes, in a sense, that's a paradox. I need help, but I resist being helped and I feel that is what she's doing, too.

**Instructor:**  That's what all clients do.

Doug really summarized the situation here, but he is unable to use his own insight, and the instructor took the focus away from him by her comment.

**Doug:**  Yeah, that's true, but she's leaving me without anything if she doesn't let me investigate or reflect. I don't know what I have left.

**Harriet:**  You feel crippled. You said it once already.

**Instructor:**  That's what you have left.

**Doug:**  What!! Feeling crippled!

**Instructor:**  Yes, that is your therapeutic tool, the knowledge of what she is doing to you.

The instructor has been trying to indicate to Doug that he is right in the middle of the thing he has been groping for and that he needs only to look at it clearly. Doug has caught a glimpse of it, as evidenced by his strong reaction, but he cannot yet fully grasp it. His next statement is made as if nothing had reached him.

**Doug:**  I don't know what she'll do on Tuesday. I guess I'm preparing myself for it, because I feel somehow she'll bring it in.

**Instructor:**  Bring what in?

**Doug:**  She'll say, "I guess I wasn't cooperating," or something like that.

**Carl:**  Why would she do that?

**Doug:**  Because I think she would half-ass deal with the issue

and drop it, and then resist. I think there is this pattern, like—
we state terms and then we kind of don't follow them and then
we—

**Instructor:**   Who is "we"?

**Doug:**   Well, I'm obviously dancing with her. I want to be cautious and try to reinforce the terms and stick to them.

**Allan:**   But the terms are that she is not to bring any defenses
or resistances?

**Ellen:**   She has to come in healthy; no sickness allowed.

**Fran:**   She came in saying she wanted to feel more and you
said that whatever you could say to her she had already thought
out and it seemed to me that you had only an intellectual
avenue of relating to her. And yet it seems that doesn't work
either; that if she isn't more aware of her feelings, she can't talk
intellectually and make any sense.

**Doug:**   In asking her to write things, I wanted to give her some
structure. She was thinking introspectively in a way that made
good literature, but not very effective problem solving.

**Gail:**   So you're reinforcing the introspective literature.

         Gail has put her finger on a major part of the trouble,
namely, the intellectualization engaged in by the therapist as
well as the client, but Doug cannot hear her.

**Doug:**   No, I was going to start with that and then begin shaping ways of thinking more systematically about the problems.
That was the strategy. I wanted to start with something she was
good at, something she would kind of like doing, and work up
from there.

**Allan:**   I still see the contract as an intellectual way of pulling
loose ends together and her coming in with the written sheets to
talk from is also a purely intellectual way of communicating
with you. The important thing is how she feels.

**Harriet:**   There is also a threat of rejection, isn't there? You're threatening that you won't concern yourself with her unless she conforms. As Allan said, the feelings have to be the crux of the therapeutic experience.

**Bob:** It seems to me that the whole area of her problems is so broad you don't know where to take it. She doesn't say what she wants to "feel something" *about*.

**Carl:** I wonder what would happen if you said to her, "You seem to have good ability to think for yourself and to see a lot of things. I wonder what it is you want from me right now." And then you might get her to define it herself in the session.

**Fran:** Maybe she wanted you to help her separate from her present boyfriend, the way she went to a psychiatrist before to help her decide to leave her husband.

**Doug:** No. When she first came, maybe, but that's not the issue now.

**Ellen:** I wonder if she still really wants to come to see you.

**Gail:** The way you describe her as having this tremendous intellectual capacity and insight—that's the thing you seem to be fascinated by.

**Doug:** No, that's not what—

**Gail:** That's what comes out when you talk about her. I'm wondering if you're not unwittingly reinforcing her intellectualizing.

Doug is taking in nothing that is being said, and the seminar is not addressing itself to his concern. The instructor was silent for some time, unable to see any way to help. Finally she tries another tack.

**Instructor:** It's really very interesting. The seminar is doing just what this girl does.

**Doug:** What the girl does?

**Instructor:** Yes. Doug is being crippled. He can't function. Most of the things that people have been saying in the seminar have been very good, showing intellectual insight into this and that; but the total effect is that Doug cannot function. Everything is scattered. Somebody says something good over here and somebody else says something good over there, but the second thing is not related to the first thing, and Doug is not helped. The effect on Doug is crippling. It is very interesting to see the mirroring that is occurring, in that the seminar is doing to him what the girl does, and he seems to be feeling the same way that he does with her—paralyzed, maimed.*

**Allan:**   Or maybe Doug is doing to us what he does to the girl.

**Instructor:**   Yes, I think that is true, too.

**Doug:**   I'm trying to reflect what I am doing with the client.

**Instructor:**   Yes, but please note, the seminar does not always behave in this way. It is in response to the particular presentation. Now, if we try, we can use this to help us understand. Doug has a very difficult patient. Six therapists have failed with her already. He is feeling put on the spot by her and by us. He wants help, but can't use our scattered intellectual comments.

**Doug:**   Yes, I'm trying to figure out what I'm doing. I must have presented in a way that encourages this scattering.

**Instructor:**   I think you did and the seminar also helped you to scatter. I think we became preoccupied with what we thought was a mistake in the way you set up a written contract, and we became antagonistic to you without saying clearly enough that we thought you made a mistake. I suspect you thought so, too, but we didn't let you tell us that.

**Doug:**   It's true. I did think that was a bungle.

The air has finally been cleared by the instructor's directly calling attention to what has happened. The mood of the seminar changes.

*For another example of the phenomenon of mirroring, compare Chapter Five.

**Ellen:** I've been getting a headache since you started to present and it has gotten progressively worse. Now it's lightened a little.

**Allan:** We were all going in different directions since we didn't agree on any focus, just as the client hasn't and Doug didn't either.

**Instructor:** One interesting aspect of it is that Doug started by presenting a very clear question. Not everyone who presents does this so clearly. And what good did it do? None.

**Ellen:** I thought it was a spurious clarity. I didn't quite believe it.

**Bob:** Didn't he present a multiple question?

**Instructor:** He said, "I want to know how I am falling into her pattern."

**Doug:** Yes.

**Allan:** The frustrating thing is that we never found out what the pattern was.

**Fran:** To the extent that we as a group are acting out this client, I think what we are really saying is that we don't want to be intellectualized. We want to be responded to as human beings. My stomach is tight and I don't know how to respond.

**Doug:** I guess what is being said is that I'm playing into the intellectualizing.

Doug is now really hearing what was said to him several times before. The voices are no longer antagonistic and strained.

**Carl:** I think it takes just plain guts to throw away the props and find out how you feel about this girl. I wanted to ask you how you feel about her. Does she turn you on? Do you feel warmth toward her?

**Doug:** She evokes a lot of things. I thought the sessions *were* on a feeling level; at least I try to keep them that way. I find it very difficult to follow what is happening here with the talk about its being intellectual. It just kind of blows my mind. If the sessions are so intellectual, I really must be blind to what I am doing.

**Allan:** That's what I meant by feeling trapped. You really just castrated yourself.

**Harriet:** I'm not fully in touch with all that's been going on here. But it is clear that this girl has not been just the pride and joy of all the other therapists she has seen. No one has had any success with her. She may be invested in—I don't know—blinding people.

**Instructor:** Yes, she could be invested in crippling her therapists.

**Doug:** I guess that's so. I wanted to get off the hook by making this contract and somehow insuring against being the failure that all the others were, or at least not be blamed for it when I failed.

**Instructor:** It's a relationship in which everything you do you get crippled for. We're recommending to you that you try to catch it at the moment that it happens and bring it back to her experience. Now you've noticed, let's say, that you were being crippled. What was it that she was doing just then, and how did that come about?

**Allan:** Rather than just confronting her with the fact that she's crippling you?

**Instructor:** Yes, what is *her* experience at the moment and how did it come about? She could say, or anybody could say, "Well, I'm sorry. It was an accident that I crippled you. I just happened to be going around the corner too fast and you were in the way." So your job is to show her that it is not an accident and that *she* is doing it. This is what you sensed when you said that she *could* keep to that contract. She has the potentiality of noticing what she is doing. You have to show her that it is happening right now—not that you just happened to become crippled, but what her part in it was. It is not an easy thing to do with a person, because it will sound like criticism to her, like, "Look what a bad thing you did." If she ever does catch on to what a castrating bitch she can be, it will be like falling from a perch. She will have to have some support underneath her to hold her when she falls, because she doesn't like to feel that she is crippling somebody (even though part of her may enjoy it), any more than you like to feel yourself crippled.

**Doug:**   It's difficult to gauge how much anger she really has, and it's going to be hard work.

**Instructor:**   It's going to be hard work, because you have got to sit there and feel crippled and notice it clearly, and then work with it with her. But you have begun to notice it, and that's the important thing.

Doug and the other seminar members moved in this session from defensive antagonism toward each other to collaborative work. The crucial point seems to have come when the instructor was able to point out the mirroring that was occurring. The seminar members were behaving like the client in response to the therapist's presentation. The interpretive comment also helped them to become aware of the antagonism with which they were responding to Doug's presentation. The excerpt illustrates how a very intelligent student can become almost stupid in his inability to hear when he is attacked and his defenses go up. Nothing useful is likely to happen in this situation until the stalemate can be overcome. Once the antagonism had been worked through, the instructor could make her point and finally be heard by Doug. He could begin to use his painful experience of being "crippled" by the client in the interest of the therapeutic work.

In this chapter, the seminar dealt with a number of problems that have been encountered before, but, since the client is different each time, the problems appear in a different form. The use of intellectualization as a defense by both therapist and client has occurred before and will no doubt occur again. Doug's use of a written contract illustrates the misuse of the idea of clarifying goals. The client who has already been to a dozen therapists brings up poignantly the beginning therapist's fear of incompetence. How should he succeed when all the others have failed? The client's use of helplessness as a way to get the therapist to make decisions for her is also a familiar issue. Doug's resemblance to his client, reminiscent of Fran's problem in Chapter Four, Section 3, turns out, as in Fran's case, not to be an advantage. The students are learning that no two clients are ever the same but that underlying issues are very similar.

---

# CHAPTER 10

# TERMINATION PROBLEMS

$T$ermination is always an important and sometimes problematic part of therapy. In a situation in which student therapists are assigned to an agency for only one or two semesters, termination problems occur more frequently than in an ordinary clinic situation or in private practice, in which a client can usually continue with his therapist until his condition warrants conclusion of the treat-

188

ment. Student therapists should, of course, tell their clients at the beginning that their contract is necessarily of limited duration. But the client may forget that it has been said, so that a reminder close to the point of termination is in order. Sometimes therapists feel guilty that they are deserting their clients, especially if they are only too glad to be rid of them. Ending any relationship that has been significant is a difficult matter for most people. The implicit reminder of death is painful. Beginning therapists tend to go to extremes by either denying the significance of the relationship or exaggerating it.

The first two sections in this chapter deal with cases in which termination was dictated by external circumstances. The final excerpt in Chapter Seven, in which Ellen is about to terminate with Ben, is also a case in point, but because of the continuity it belongs more appropriately in Chapter Seven. The last two sections in this chapter deal with questions of termination dictated by internal considerations.

## Section 1
## Termination of Short-Term Therapy

This section deals with the problem of termination in short-term therapy. Fran has just presented her work with a young male client with whom one problem has been successfully resolved.

**Instructor:** I think you have another problem now, and that is ending with Henry. You must have only two or three sessions left. When you first saw him, did you make it quite clear how many sessions you could have with him?

**Fran:** Yes, I said I could see him for six weeks and then I would arrange for him to be transferred to somebody else.

**Instructor:** What is the story now about transferring?

**Fran:** I haven't asked anybody else yet on the agency staff. First Henry has to decide if he wants to go on.

**Instructor:** But don't you as a professional person want to make a recommendation? If he is quite clear that he wants to continue and you have agreed that he should, it may not be necessary to say anything more about it, but I think you would want to make it explicit that this is how it is.

**Fran:**   He was very clear about it in the beginning.

**Harriet:**   But clients do change their minds in the course of a few interviews.

**Instructor:**   Yes, you can't take for granted that he still thinks the way he did a month ago. When you are doing very short-term therapy, it is important to focus on one or two points so that he doesn't feel he's just roaming around. Then, when he stops, he feels he has accomplished something. I think you did that. The question is, what now?

**Fran:**   I'm not sure which point to focus on.

**Carl:**   You could focus on the discrepancies in his story.

**Instructor:**   I think it's important with any patient, but especially in short-term therapy, to remember, when you point out discrepancies, to give some support and understanding of how they came about. In Henry's case, he didn't have much practice in his early life in putting things together, so it's no wonder he doesn't notice discrepancies. In any case, I suggest you give some thought to what you want to concentrate on now; you might ask him to give some thought to it, too. You might also remember that it is not absolutely essential to sit out the six weeks with him. If you come to a good stopping place, that might be the time to make the transition.

The instructor is trying to emphasize that in very short-term therapy, termination must constantly be kept in mind at the same time that therapist and client focus on some aspect of the client's problem. This is another way of saying that the client must not be allowed to proceed as if he could develop a relationship with the therapist over an indefinite period of time. This is technically a difficult matter. Short-term therapy can also be very intense. It is like a short run up a hill, compared to a slow climb up a mountain of which the peak is obscured by clouds. In very short-term therapy, the end of the particular relationship is in view from the beginning. What is not known is how it looks from the brow of the hill.

### Section 2
### Too Painful To Discuss

This section illustrates the mechanism of denial as it operates in the therapist. The therapy had been quite successful, but the termination is presenting problems that the therapist would prefer to avoid. The presenter in this case is Doug, who has been seeing a twenty-two-year-old single woman for most of the academic year. She had made good progress in overcoming her timidity and is just beginning to move out of her isolation in a meaningful way.

**Instructor:** It's fine that you feel you understand her now that you are coming very close to termination, but what sounds a warning gong in my head is the hint that she is building you up as the only person who *could* understand her. Then you become irreplaceable in her life.

**Allan:** So the reinforcements the world has to offer could never match what she gets from you.

**Instructor:** Exactly, except that it's all illusory. You are *not* the only person who could understand her.

**Doug:** I don't think I've avoided confronting her.

**Gail:** You have been awfully nice to her.

**Doug:** I was hoping that my reinforcement of her effective behavior would enable her to discriminate and that she could get positive reinforcers now from her natural environment.

**Instructor:** That's fine, but don't you have to ask yourself whether that is what has happened? What satisfaction is she getting now from her environment? Or are you *the* source of satisfaction and security in her life? In the latter case, when you stop seeing her, you are leaving her very high and dry.

**Ellen:** I think she's giving out all kinds of signals that you are terribly important to her. Maybe she's hoping that you won't really leave the agency. What does she say about it?

**Doug:**   Well, I wanted to use the time to talk about her problems and not just about our relationship. I thought the other things were more important.

This is an example of a student finding it too painful to discuss the ending of the relationship and rationalizing this by finding the "other things" more important. The client also finds the subject painful and has avoided coming close to it except in oblique ways. Doug is very loath to go into his own feelings in the situation.

**Harriet:**   I don't know what could be more important at this point. How do you feel about leaving her?

**Doug:**   I don't have any choice.

Doug again shies off from the question about his own attitude, and refers to the fact that he is leaving the city for an internship elsewhere.

**Instructor:**   We often say that we have no choice when we mean that we have already made a decision about what our priorities are. The fact is that, if this woman were important enough to you, you could stay here and continue to see her and not take the internship you were offered. Please understand, I am not saying that you ought to do this. I am simply wanting to point out to you that you do or did have a choice and you made it. If she gets the message that she is not top priority in your life, she is perfectly right. But what we are all concerned about, I think, is that you may be top priority at this moment in her life and that is not being talked about and worked through while you still have time to do it.

**Bob:**   I stopped with a client recently because she went away, and I had the sudden thought, "Now I know what my mother went through when I first went off to college."

**Ellen:**   I know what you mean.

**Allan:**   I do, too.

**Doug:** Well, it's funny. I did think of my mother when she left the session last time, and I thought she started to cry as she was going out of the room.

**Harriet:** It's really better for her if you can talk about it. It's terrible if she has to cry about it alone.

**Doug:** I guess you're right. I wanted to avoid it.

It now appears that Doug was not as unaware as he would like to be that there are very strong feelings involved in the termination, both on his part and on the part of his client. The theme of desertion is difficult, since students themselves often feel guilty about having deserted their parents and perhaps others as well and do not want to be reminded of it. Doug can begin to work with the problem now that other seminar members have offered him the support of their own similar experience.

It is not necessary to go into the details of this case in order to make clear the point that often troubles beginning therapists who are ending a good therapeutic relationship. So many young Americans have been brought up to expect happy endings that it is not surprising to find them reluctant to experience the pain of separation. It is usually even more difficult for them to bring this pain into the open with clients when, in addition, they feel guilt about deserting someone still in need of a supportive relationship.

### Section 3
### Avoidance of a Troublesome Issue

This section and the next illustrate problems about termination of a different kind. Therapy is not being ended by the external circumstance of the student therapist leaving the agency, but by internal factors of the relationship. When termination is brought about by external factors, therapist and client have to do the best they can within limits set by reality. Sometimes this experience can be used to help a client face other kinds of limits set by such things as a physical handicap or separation, through death or some other external circumstance, from someone to whom he is attached. When the termination is not forced from the outside, the client is not learning about adapting gracefully to fate but about making a decision in which he can have a major role, along with his therapist. The responsibility of the therapist may be greater when he and the client have a choice to make, and the range of mistakes that can be made seems to be wider.

In this section, the client is talking about stopping therapy before it seems advisable. The difficulty for the seminar lies in helping the therapist, Fran, to see that she wants to do what she says she is afraid of doing. The client is a young man who is quite extraordinary in the number of assets he possesses. He is handsome, charming, a football hero, and a graduate summa cum laude from a prominent university. At the time of the case presentation, he is a law student, doing well in school and promising to be a successful lawyer. The problem for which he had come to therapy centered on his four-year-old marriage to a girl who had been his high school sweetheart and who seems not to have kept pace with his development. She has refused to enter therapy herself, either alone or together with her husband. After some months of therapeutic work with Fran, the marriage had become less of a battlefield but was rather empty. This was not the first time the seminar has heard about the case. Fran has just been presenting her most recent work with the client, called John.

**Fran:**  The entire session we focused on John's tendency to intellectualize whenever I questioned his feelings, particularly toward me. He said that I brought out a lot of positive feelings in him that he was afraid of right now. Then he told me I was a threat to him because I brought back a lot of the pain that he was usually able to forget.

**Doug:**  Was he feeling that your relationship with him threatens his marriage?

**Fran:**  I asked him that and he said yes. He said settling down in marriage takes a lot of hard work, that it's an active process, and that he is usually passive in relationships to women though he is active in his work. I said, "I think you want our relationship to be genuine, but it's hard to believe that it could be." He said he is hung up because our relationship is a one-sided one. I can do things for him, but there is very little he can do for me. I said, "I hear you saying you're wanting to give. Why not? Why do you see yourself as non-giving in here?" He said it was because the focus was on him and it was not an equal relationship. I said, "Equal?" And he said, 'Yes, we're not dealing with the problems you have. And I don't have much to offer you."

**Instructor:** Before we go any further, is there anything special in the relationship, Fran, that you would like us to concentrate on?

The instructor senses that there is a countertransference problem and hopes that Fran will bring it into the discussion, but she does not go after it directly, and Fran does not follow up on it.

**Fran:** I have some question about termination of therapy. I really don't think he's ready, but he had said the session before last that he wanted to stop. I'm not sure if I'm taking him deeper into therapy than he originally wanted to go, deeper than he contracted for. He says he's getting along better with his wife; he's more at ease in social situations. So, why shouldn't I be satisfied? But I'm not. I can see he has a lot he's holding back on with me. But I'm not sure I can—I'm not sure I should manipulate him to stay on. I just don't know if I have the right to do that.

The seminar discusses the problem of termination but misses the full force of Fran's use of the phrase "can . . . should manipulate him" in this connection.

**Gail:** You ask whether you have the right to ask him to stay in therapy. Does that imply some ambivalence in your earlier statement that you think he is in need of more therapy? I'm suggesting that, if you were really convinced that he needed it, you would come out and tell him so.

**Fran:** I'm convinced he should remain in therapy longer, but he's saying he wants to stop. He claims he just has a little problem dealing with one of his professors whom he has to see soon, and if he could just get over his anger at him everything would be all right. I don't know if all this is resistance or whether he's really telling me that he doesn't want to be in therapy. Now, don't laugh.

**Instructor:** I wasn't laughing. I'm baffled. He's got two legs that he can walk out of that room on any time he wants to. Also, he's very articulate and can tell you a lot about himself.

**Allan:** I don't understand why you're asking us. Ask him.

**Instructor:** Gail, did you get your question answered?

**Gail:** I still wonder why you don't tell him what you think.

**Fran:** I really don't know why I didn't.

**Instructor:** You must feel something that's keeping you from making a clear statement of your own position. Then he would, of course, be free to stay, come, or go. You can't make him stay. You *may* be able to manipulate him. I find myself puzzled about your use of that word. I don't have any quarrel with your opinion that he should continue, but I'm wondering why you are having trouble with it.

**Fran:** I'm really in a bind. There's a lot of upheaval going on in him, I think. Somebody once told me that if you break down the word *therapist* you get *the rapist*. I don't want to do that. I wonder if we have the right to cause that much disruption in the person's marriage or work. Often people find when they've gotten rid of the aggravating things in their lives, they're not left with too much else either.

In hindsight it seems very clear that Fran is struggling with her own suppressed wish to keep this young man for herself, to "rape" him, "manipulate" him, and so on, into leaving his wife and being with her and for her. At this point, however, the seminar members, including the instructor, become caught up somewhat moralistically in problems of role and responsibility and miss the main point. Their language betrays their preoccupation with a sexual relationship.

**Ellen:** I think our profession presents the ultimate kind of challenge. We really have enormous power over our clients. The challenge is not to misuse it. You are feeling powerful enough to really screw John up.

**Bob:** I was thinking of that exact point. There are two R's, the right and responsibility in the role. What do you feel your role should be? John seems to be going in and out of the client role.

**Fran:** I think he's looking at me and saying to himself, "I wonder what it would be like with her," what a real relationship would be with me.

Fran is not addressing herself to Bob's question because she is not yet able to become aware of her own feelings, but she is again giving very strong clues about her impulses that the seminar does not follow up.

**Harriet:** I wish I knew a little bit more about the course of his life. It sounds like he got into this marriage very young because he felt he could take care of this girl and that would bring something good out in him. But things have actually been pretty depressing. The marriage sounds empty even if it is now more bearable. He may feel terribly guilty about the whole thing.

**Instructor:** Guilty because he doesn't want to be there, right?

**Carl:** If he did make some critical decisions like changing the conditions of his marriage or staying in therapy, would you see that as a potential stress for you?

**Fran:** I don't know if I want to be an agent of all that.

**Carl:** You're talking about him as if he were just a little kid.

**Instructor:** Or a robot. You push the buttons and he makes the moves. You don't let him assume the responsibility for making changes himself.

**Fran:** Oh, I do. I very definitely think he can do things for himself. But I think his feelings about doing all these things are so caught up with me that they have been distorted.

Fran is now saying clearly that John's trouble lies in his feelings toward her, but she has not yet uncovered the difficulty in her feelings toward him.

**Doug:** You're saying he'll do things like getting a divorce because of you?

**Ellen:** As if you were able to seduce him in some way.

**Instructor:** I think we have to be very respectful of the feeling Fran has that she could affect him. She has a choice to make in how she will treat him, and she doesn't like that.

The instructor has attempted to give Fran enough support to allow her to see more clearly what she is defending against in herself, but it does not work; the discussion moves off again on a tangent.

**Harriet:** I get the picture that ever since his marriage things have been terrible for him. Before that, he was a happy kid and he wasn't feeling so pinned down.

**Allan:** You said the marriage was improving, and I'm wondering what you're feeling now about how it improved. Or is it just that he wrote it off more?

**Fran:** This is conjecture, but I think the marriage is probably better. I don't have any information.

**Instructor:** But isn't that very strange that you don't have information about this very important matter that was his reason for seeing you in the first place?

The instructor is sounding rather irritated here, since it seems to be impossible to get at Fran's blind spot and since information is lacking on such a central issue. Other seminar members also show some irritation that does not move the discussion any further.

**Carl:** He's sort of playing a cat-and-mouse seductive game with you, as I see it.

**Ellen:** Have you said that to him?

**Fran:** Oh, yes. We've talked about that. I brought it up in the last session. I asked him if he really enjoyed teasing me, and he said, "It's more comfortable for me to do that than to get serious."

Fran has now formulated the problem quite clearly, but only in terms of the client. In the interviews with him, she is avoiding the subject of his marriage. She is suggesting that her relationship to him could well be "real," suggesting that he has things to "give" her, and in general making herself attractive and semiavailable, while at the same time outwardly keeping the appropriate professional proprieties. He is responding in kind, talking about stopping the professional relationship while making it quite clear that he has some unfinished business with her.

**Gail:** I get the feeling that there is something else bothering you about your relationship with him. When you were talking, the tone of your voice was kind of defensive, as if you were trying to protect what was going on there from us.

**Fran:** I had the feeling last night when I was working on the notes for presenting today that something had happened in the last session. I was very conscious of that. After I wrote out all the notes I was left with the feeling there was something else going on that I can't get hold of.

**Allan:** On the tape your responses are kind of abstract, too. It just sounds as though there's something you feel you have to protect, something that's going on there.

**Doug:** What if his marriage is dissolved?

**Fran:** I think I would be very uncomfortable. I know I would be.

**Instructor:** Why? Marriages have dissolved before. It's not such an unusual thing.

The instructor has tried to get Fran to look at what her part in the dissolution of the marriage would be, but the question is too indirect; it does not work.

**Fran:**   I know, but I'm not sure it's a case of their not being right for each other. He may be doing a lot of things in this marriage that he would do in the next, and I guess it would be more my intent to help him see what he's doing rather than to dissolve the marriage.

**Bob:**   But why would you feel uncomfortable if *he* made the decision?

**Fran:**   I don't. I'd just feel uncomfortable if the marriage were dissolved.

Fran mishears Bob's question, which indicates that there is a lot of stress around this point. Her suppressed wish to see him get away from his wife and devote himself to her has become clearer and clearer.

**Doug:**   I'm wondering the same thing as Bob. Why do you think you have the power to direct his life?

**Fran:**   I don't feel I have the power, but I'm afraid he's going to jump out of the marriage too quickly.

**Harriet:**   That implies that you have some expectation of what he should do or what he shouldn't do.

**Instructor:**   And that you know when "too quickly" is. I think Doug's point is important that you are taking upon yourself more power, and I might also say more omniscience, than you really have. It's not up to you to decide whether or when he should break up his marriage. You have the responsibility of clarifying but not making decisions.

Here the instructor has fallen into the trap of sermonizing at Fran rather than trying to get at what she is hiding from herself. Ellen in her next intervention puts her finger on the sore point.

**Ellen:**   I think you might have got worried when he told you that you are not as nondirective as you think you are. That implies you really are telling him what to do, even though you don't think you are.

**Fran:** Yes, that remark of his did give me a chill, and I thought I would have to be very careful not to. . . .

Fran's voice trails off, and she pauses. The seminar members wisely let the pause continue, and this time Fran breaks through her own defenses.

**Fran:** I think I'm afraid I will influence him to leave his wife. I do like him very much. I know it's a terrible thing to say about another human being, but she has never seemed to me to be good enough for John and she doesn't appreciate him.

**Ellen:** It's not really surprising. You've made him sound to me like a very attractive character with all kinds of potential, both intellectual and emotional. It's not really surprising that you would want him for yourself, especially when his wife seems so indifferent to him.

**Fran:** But I shouldn't influence him. I shouldn't let him see.

**Instructor:** I think these things are more controllable when you are highly aware of them. These impulses have power over you as long as they are hidden. They lose their power in the clear light of day. Then you can use your positive feelings toward him in the service of the therapy, to help him to free himself from the chains he has put on himself. I don't mean external chains supplied by his wife, but the ones of his own making.

**Carl:** I got a similar kind of picture of him as a very strong guy standing in a basket trying to pick it up.

**Fran:** That's true. He does seem strong, but he's using his strength in a futile struggle against himself. He just needs to step out of the basket. I guess I really want that for him more than I want him for myself. I think now I could tell him with a good conscience that he should not stop therapy.

Fran has finally been able to recognize her hidden impulses and to see the possibility of using them in John's interest. If this had not been the case, it would have been better to transfer this client to another therapist. When therapists use their clients for the satisfaction of their personal needs, the clients are unlikely to profit. The more positive aspects a client has, the more likely he is unwittingly to seduce a therapist to misuse him. This is a particular danger for young therapists with clients of the opposite sex. In this case, the tendency to idealize John stood in the way of Fran's seeing clearly the neurotic aspect of his personality. She in turn led the seminar to idealize him, so that it became quite difficult to perceive his need for therapy. Instead, it sometimes appeared that he was simply in the wrong marriage and the therapist could develop the hidden fantasy that the "right woman" (who would, of course, be herself) would fix everything up for him. In subsequent hours she was able to help the client to see the self-destructive aspects of his patterns of relating to women in general.

This case is an example of a client who proposes stopping therapy in order to avoid a difficult issue. If the therapist is aware of this, it is relatively simple to point it out to the client and to help him to face and work through the difficulty. The trouble in this case lay in the fact that the therapist also wanted to avoid the issue and was, therefore, not able to be firm and unconflicted in her opinion that the client should continue. She thought she was afraid that he might leave his wife, a development that would make her feel guilty and might not do him any good. More deeply, she wished that he would leave his wife and thus be free to enter into a personal relationship with her. When she was able to see clearly that her fear concealed her wish, she was able to be free of the fear and to reduce the wish to manageable proportions. The seminar members learned that they would do well to question their hidden motives when they found themselves conflicted about a client's proposal to terminate.

## Section 4
## Premature Termination

This section illustrates how easy it is for therapists to be misled into thinking that their clients are ready to stop therapy when, actually, important issues have not yet been touched.

Doug is telling the seminar that he had started to cut down the number of sessions with his client with the idea that termination was at hand. In the discussion that followed Doug's presentation, some of the dynamics in the situation became clear. The client is a young unmarried woman in her late twenties who had led a rather unstable life both in terms of career and in terms of personal relationships. During the five months she had been in therapy, she had been more successful in keeping a job and had apparently developed quite a stable relationship with one man. Doug has just been reporting to the seminar his decision, to which the client had seemed to agree, that they should meet only every two weeks. He had also told her that they would probably soon terminate.

**Doug:** (Speaking with some disappointment.) And then she came in yesterday and she had clearly been drinking too much. She said it turned out that the man she had been going with was married. She goofed off and didn't go to work, and she knows that endangers her job.

**Bob:** Had she known before that he was married?

**Doug:** It isn't quite clear. She may have guessed. I didn't ask her. But now he is saying things like he has to go home early because of his wife and he can't spend the weekend with her, and so forth. I really felt angry at him. She has been rejected so many times, and I wanted things to go well for her.

**Instructor:** Was she angry at him?

**Doug:** Well, a little bit, not as much as I would have thought. She was just wondering whether she should go on seeing him.

**Instructor:** It seems as if *you* are doing the feeling for your client.

**Allan:** I think I would be angry, too, if I were Doug. The client has improved a lot and now this guy seems to destroy it all. He put her right back where she was a few months ago.

**Instructor:** You think he is responsible for this?

**Gail:**   I think it is very convenient to blame it on him.

**Ellen:**   I agree. Then neither Doug nor the client needs to look at their part in it.

**Doug:**   (Laughing defensively.) I don't see what my part is. *I* didn't tell her I was married and couldn't spend the weekend with her.

**Instructor:**   It could be that cutting her down to half the number of interviews is about the same thing from her point of view.

**Doug:**   (Suddenly serious again.) Oh, I see what you mean.

It is quite striking that Doug has not made the connection himself between cutting down the hours and the client's behavior in drinking too much and not getting to work. How the boyfriend's behavior fits in is unclear, since she has let it remain obscure whether she knew about his marriage earlier or not. (It appeared in later interviews that she had really known it all along, but had preferred not to think about it.) Both Doug and the client are finding a convenient scapegoat in the boyfriend. The real threat lies in cutting off the therapeutic relationship. Doug has claimed that he broached the subject of termination because the client gave so much evidence of improvement. It remains for the seminar to question this.

**Harriet:**   I thought you were awfully quick to cut down the number of sessions when she showed the first signs of being better. There wasn't any external pressure on you from your agency to do this and I wondered why you were so eager to be rid of her.

**Doug:**   I didn't think of it that way. I was respecting her wish for independence.

**Instructor:**   That sounds very reasonable, but let us ask you to think carefully whether and when you felt anxious in the recent sessions with her before you cut down the hours.

**Doug:**   Well, she brought in some poems she had written and wanted me to read them. I did read them, but I didn't know what to say. I felt quite uncomfortable. I'm not a literary critic.

**Gail:** What were they about?

**Doug:** They were sort of love poems.

**Gail:** She put you on the spot, didn't she?

**Doug:** I didn't think of it that way. I didn't realize it at the time.

**Gail:** I think she was indirectly feeling you out, to see if you would respond to her as a lover. She was making very strong demands on you.

**Instructor:** At the same time she was flattering you by indicating what a fine therapist you are. Her symptoms improved markedly.

**Doug:** That's what I was paying attention to.

**Instructor:** It's very understandable that you should wish to get out of this uncomfortable situation in which she is making very strong unspoken demands on you—to be her lover and her father and everything else. She miscalculated, unconsciously, when she showed so much improvement. Her apparent stability was based on her relationship to you. I don't mean to say that she did all this consciously. If she had been aware of what she was doing, she might not have agreed to cut down her hours. She had to go along with your suggestion in order to please you.

**Doug:** Well, I guess I did rush the termination.

**Instructor:** It's not a bad rule of thumb to let your clients bring up the matter of termination first, unless there are external reasons why you have to stop the therapy.

**Gail:** Then they can't feel rejected, can they?

**Instructor:** Well, it is remarkable how clients can turn all kinds of things into rejection. But it is true that there's less chance of it if they bring it up first. Of course they may bring the subject up in order to test you out or to avoid going the next step into some painful material. But you can help them to evaluate whether these are the real reasons or not.

**Ellen:**   I had the experience once of agreeing with a client's wish to terminate. She stopped and after two weeks she was back again more anxious than ever.

**Doug:**   Well, that's what has happened with this woman essentially. Only we didn't actually terminate.

**Instructor:**   It may well be that you can use the whole episode constructively to help her see what she is doing to you and to others.

It has become clear to Doug and to the other seminar members that termination, actual or imagined, can be used to avoid going through some difficult material that causes anxiety in the therapist or client or both. In this case Doug was able to correct the mistake and to work through his anxiety about the demands that his client was unconsciously making upon him. As in the preceding section, Doug was blind to the important issue, namely the personal involvement of the client with the therapist. In this case it is easier than it was for Fran, since Doug himself is less entangled. But he is trying to avoid bringing up the issue of the client's dependence on him by premature termination.

When no external circumstances dictate ending, it requires considerable clinical judgment to know when to terminate therapy and to do it skillfully. The rule of thumb advocated by the instructor is generally a good one. But, as she pointed out, the fact that a client talks about termination may need investigation rather than simple acquiescence. It may be a way of finding out whether the therapist is willing to take the plunge into a deeper level of discourse or into some seemingly dangerous topics. It may be a way to avoid bringing up difficult material. The therapist must learn to listen to the client's tone of voice as well as to his words to be able to judge what the hidden messages may be. If he is not in too much of a hurry to come to a decision, it will usually become clear whether the client is really hoping the therapist will say no to his desires to escape or whether he is taking a significant step toward independence.

# CHAPTER 11

# THE SOCIAL SYSTEM IN WHICH THE THERAPIST OPERATES

**B**eginning therapists, concerned as they must be with the one-to-one relationship with their clients, often forget that the social system in which they operate—for example, the agency, clinic, or school in which they work—is inevitably an important aspect of the relationship. They know whether they like their working conditions, their bosses, their coworkers, and the secretaries who make their appointments, but they often fail to realize the impact of these attitudes upon their work with clients. Conversely, they may fail to realize that the attitudes of their clients toward the agency in question have something to do with the clients' attitudes toward therapy and toward therapists as representatives of the agency.

## Section 1
## The Influence of Low Status

The following excerpt illustrates the way in which one aspect of a social system adversely affected the interaction between the therapist, Harriet, and her client, Alice.

**Harriet:**   My client, Alice, had a hard time getting started the last time I saw her. Finally she began to talk about how it felt to be the youngest in her family, with four siblings all of whom were more than seven years older than she was. "Sure it had a few advantages to be the baby," she said, "but mostly I felt like a second-class citizen. I wonder if you ever get over that." I was kind of curious about what brought her around to that topic. But before I could ask she switched, I thought, to one of her teachers who has only adjunct status in the university and who doesn't have an office where he can see people. Alice thinks he is an okay teacher, but she wonders if she is being given an unfair deal by being assigned to somebody so low in the hierarchy. When she asks him for a letter of recommendation at the end of the year, it won't count for much, at least not for as much as if the letter came from a full professor. Suddenly I realized that we had been put out of our usual meeting place that day. We had been about to begin our session when one of the senior psychiatrists came in and claimed his office. I had to ask Alice to wait a minute while I found another place. It really was just a minute and I had forgotten about it. But then I saw the connection.

Harriet pauses in her account and seems reluctant to go on.

**Gail:**   What did you do then?

**Harriet:**   Well, that's the trouble. I didn't do anything. I was thinking how I am a second-class citizen in that agency and only have adjunct status, so to speak, and anyone can put me out of an office any time they want. Alice was wandering on, talking about something, and I was scarcely listening. Finally, I sort of blurted out, probably quite irrelevantly at the moment, "I guess you're concerned about my low status here, aren't you?" She looked surprised and asked what I meant. By that time I didn't know whether I was mad at her for bringing it up and then denying it, or at the agency for putting me in that position, or at myself for not handling it better. But for sure I was irritated at somebody.

**Doug:**   I don't blame you. I get the same treatment in the agency where I work and it makes me mad as hell.

**Instructor:**   I think the important thing to notice here is how you may take these feelings out on your clients, to be sure, unintentionally and unwittingly, but just the same they come out. Harriet might have been able to handle the situation with Alice much more effectively if she had let herself know and become familiar with her own feelings about the agency long before the particular incident occurred.

**Ellen:**   That's a problem I don't have with my agency. I think the paraprofessionals have managed to impress on the psychiatrists and other high-status people that they need to be treated with respect, and students in all the professions profit from that.

**Instructor:**   It's too bad that a lot of mental health agencies don't take into consideration the mental health of all their employees. But pecking orders are significant in most human institutions. I think that within the pecking order it is quite possible to treat the lowest as well as the highest with respect. Ellen's agency is an example of that. But it is not always done. You can see how important it is for you to be aware of the system in which you are working for your client's sake as well as your own. If you can't change it, you can at least try to compensate for its weaknesses.

The instructor has summarized the essential lesson of this excerpt. It is striking that Harriet had practically forgotten about the incident that precipitated the difficulty in her session with the client. She was so used to being treated as a second-class citizen in her agency that being put out of her accustomed meeting place had almost gone unnoticed. Clearly, it had impressed the client, however, who quite unwittingly finds round-about ways of referring to what has obviously been a significant event. To be sure, it fits Alice's pathology to feel that she is low on the totem pole. Harriet, who is surer of herself, can more easily overlook the slight, but she would have done well to notice that the significance was not lost upon her client.

## Section 2
## The Client Who is Disrespectful of the Clinic

In this excerpt, the client's misuse of and disrespect for people, including herself, could have been noticed immediately in her attitude toward the system with which she was making an initial contact, namely the clinic. The client, like those presented in Chapter Four, elicits negative feelings on the part of her therapist of which he was at first unaware. This is an important part of the learning in the seminar session. But the additional and really central issue in this case is one that often goes unnoticed by experienced as well as inexperienced therapists, namely, the therapist's role as a representative of a social system.

The client in this excerpt is a young woman, recently divorced, employed as a secretary, whose first presenting complaint was that she could not get used to her status as a single woman. However, she did not focus on this but talked about her difficulties in meeting her parents' expectations of her. The therapist, Allan, maintained that he liked his client, but was uncertain how he ought to respond to her. He has had just one interview with her and is sharing with the seminar his doubts about how to proceed.

**Allan:**   On the one hand she was telling me she was worthless, incompetent, and useless. Her marriage was a failure, and she hasn't found any other man who has become really interested in her. But, on the other hand, she seemed to take great pleasure in beating the system. She seemed to enjoy telling me how she had cheated on exams in high school and in college and got good grades that way. Then she told me she had shoplifted and never been caught. At first I felt sympathetic with her, and then I didn't know what to think.

**Gail:**    You probably felt sympathetic with the part of her that feels worthless, but the clever side of her is not so nice.

**Ellen:**    I was wondering how much she is manipulating you.

**Doug:**    And lying to you, too.

**Allan:**    I did wonder if she was embroidering a bit, but I didn't think she was lying. She's had a pretty hard life.

The seminar members are more aware than Allan himself of the negative feelings that this young woman arouses in others. He is emphasizing the sad aspects of her life, which do indeed exist, but which are serving to obscure to him how much the client had manipulated him and how uncomfortable and resentful this had made him. He is trying to maintain an image of himself as the always helpful, always sympathetic therapist.

**Harriet:**    When you played part of the tape, she was complaining and complaining about her father's cruelty and harshness toward her, but she somehow didn't seem to be experiencing any pain about it.

**Allan:**    But he was really awful. He beat her for the tiniest little infraction of his rules.

**Bob:**    You mean, she couldn't beat *his* system.

**Allan:**    She said her father loved her, but he didn't like her.

**Instructor:**    Do you think she feels the same way about him?

**Allan:**    I guess so. She certainly talked a lot about him and he still has an enormous influence on her, but she doesn't say anything good about him.

**Instructor:** Did anything strike you as strange about this family?

**Allan:** I don't understand what you mean.

**Instructor:** Well, you presented for 45 minutes. You talked and she talked a lot about her family, but her mother was not mentioned once. First it was all about her father, and then she said "they" quite a few times, referring to her parents. But the mother appears to be a zero; she's not mentioned once by herself. Did you ask your client about that?

**Allan:** No, I didn't. I felt I shouldn't press to obtain more information. I wanted her to see that I was more interested in what was important to her, rather than in what was important to me or what I was just curious about.

**Instructor:** It's hard to imagine that a girl's mother wouldn't be important to her. If she hadn't talked about her family at all, okay, that would be one thing. She might have something else very pressing on her mind that she needed to get out in the first interview. But she did talk a great deal about her childhood. People who aren't mentioned are usually very significant, when they have obviously played important roles. Is it possible that this father, harsh as he may have been, was at least reliable, and that the mother was not? Maybe she is more like Mother, cheating and stealing and also manipulating? I know you've had only one interview with her, but do you have any information on how she has behaved about setting up appointments?

**Allan:** She made two appointments before she actually came in. She broke one without cancelling; one she called up and cancelled without giving any reason, and then she came in for the third.

**Instructor:** Did you talk with her about all that?

**Allan:** No, I didn't. It had all happened before I had any contact with her. It was all handled by the receptionist in the clinic.

**Instructor:** Any thoughts about that now?

**Allan:**   Maybe I should have mentioned it, but she had other things she wanted to talk about. It was before she had any contact with me, so I didn't think it had to do with me.

**Instructor:**   I think you glossed over an aspect of this client's attitude toward therapy because supposedly it did not relate to you personally. You overlooked that you *are* a part of the clinic and you are perceived as such by the client. Your virtues and your mistakes are its virtues and its mistakes. Conversely, its virtues and mistakes are yours. You can be sure that the clients will experience this and respond to it. Sometimes a client may try to drive a wedge between the therapist and his agency as a child may try to drive a wedge between his parents, especially if he feels the bonds between them to be fragile. But in any case you can be sure that he will experience you as part of a system; he will probably know this better than you do yourself. The way a client treats the agency is a good indication of what his attitude is toward you.

Allan's overlooking the client's behavior in this respect is part of his defense against becoming aware of his own negative attitudes toward her. His discomfort about his work with her becomes more acute as the discussion proceeds and as the other seminar members voice their own negative feelings.

**Ellen:**   I bet you'll have trouble with her about future appointments.

**Carl:**   It's like she pulled the wool over your eyes the way she did with her professors who gave her good grades.

**Bob:**   I think she's obnoxious. I don't think I would like her as a client.

**Allan:**   I like working with her and I don't find her obnoxious.

**Carl:**   When I was presenting one of my clients one time, a number of people here expressed dislike for him. I could only think of helping him as best I could when I was with him and I didn't see the qualities that some of you disliked—especially you, Allan—but afterward I did, and it helped me to see how he got into so much trouble with other people. I think you have some gut feelings about this woman that you don't admit.

Carl has succinctly put into words the stumbling block that kept Allan from dealing more effectively with his client and gave rise to his many doubts about what he ought to do. It is important to note that Carl and Allan were in very good rapport with each other at this time, so that Carl could say things to him with impunity that other seminar members could not. Carl also prefaced his punch line by a reminder to Allan of a time when the roles had been reversed. There is a short silence while Allan thinks about what has been said.

**Allan:** When people come in and say they are insecure or anxious or something like that, I sort of know what to do. But when she began almost gloating about getting away with cheating and stealing I felt surprised. And I guess the truth is that I didn't like it. Maybe that's moralistic and I tried not to be judgmental, but I didn't like it. If I hadn't been her therapist, I would have said I didn't like it.

**Carl:** I think we try sometimes so hard to be professional that we fall over backward. We do have spontaneous reactions to people and they are important whether we like it or not.

**Ellen:** Maybe she was trying to shock you to try you out and see what you would do.

**Allan:** Well, I guess I didn't do anything. I was debating with myself whether it was more important to stop her and ask questions, or try to interpret, or to let her continue saying whatever came to her mind.

**Instructor:** I think that is a difficult decision to make and you can't always expect to make it correctly. I think, if a client told me that he is in the habit of practicing conscious deception, that I would say at some point—I don't know how to tell you at what point—"Well, you and I have a problem together, because I can't be of as much use to you as I could otherwise be when I have to keep thinking that you may just now be lying to me or deceiving me in some way. And probably you will sometimes succeed in deceiving me, which won't exactly be to your benefit. The only thing we can do now is to be aware that this is a problem between us and to try to notice how it works."

**Allan:**    I think I could do that the next time.

Unfortunately, there was no next time. The client did not appear for her next interview, and routine attempts at follow-up by the agency elicited no response. In hindsight, the seminar developed the hypothesis that Ellen had been right in thinking the client was trying Allan out and had decided that he would let her get away with too much. Or it may have been that she found the work of therapy was going to be more than she had bargained for.

The client's failure to respond to a polite letter of inquiry from the clinic about whether she wished to continue or discontinue her interviews is in line with her earlier disrespect for the clinic in not bothering to keep her appointments. This was surely an important part of her psychodynamics that went unnoticed and that conceivably could have been used to good purpose in the initial interview with her.

The two sections of this chapter illustrate the importance to the therapist of recognizing the fact that he is embedded in a social system that has particular characteristics and to which he and his client respond in particular ways. The private practitioner, too, will find that he identifies himself or is identified by his clients as being part of a system. He belongs to a school of thought. He is a member of a professional organization and affiliated with one or the other agency. This is part of his image, just as his sex, his age, his physical characteristics, and his office furniture are also part of his image and are playing a role, conscious or unconscious, in the relationships between him and his clients.

CHAPTER 12

𝔯𝔯𝔯𝔯𝔯𝔯𝔯𝔯𝔯𝔯𝔯𝔯𝔯𝔯𝔯𝔯𝔯𝔯𝔯𝔯𝔯𝔯𝔯𝔯𝔯𝔯𝔯𝔯𝔯𝔯𝔯𝔯𝔯𝔯𝔯𝔯

# ANTITHERAPEUTIC ASPECTS OF THE SEMINAR

The term *iatrogenic*, meaning "induced by treatment," is used in psychiatry to refer to ailments that are brought about by the fact of treatment by a physician, no doubt unwittingly and unwillingly as far as the physician is concerned. These ailments may be "imaginary" in the sense that no organic basis can be found for them, but they are real enough to the patient. The fact of treatment by a physi-

216

cian may, for example, suggest to a patient that he "ought to be ill"—otherwise, the presence of the physician makes no sense.

Analogously in this seminar, ailments of the learning process were induced by the seminar itself and in particular by the presence of the instructor. The physician's wish to induce cure and the teacher's wish to induce learning are no protection against these disorders. In the seminar they sprang from the very center of the learning process. These antitherapeutic aspects of the seminar, as we called them, have been referred to briefly in previous chapters. The term *antitherapeutic* might mean two things. It could refer to the vain hope on the part of students that the seminar would be a pleasant curative experience for them, which it did not turn out to be. But, more importantly, it meant that the very existence of the seminar functioned antithetically to the best interest of the clients, in that the students acted untherapeutically by virtue of their membership in the seminar. The examples below, from four different sessions, are typical and poignant.

The first example followed on a presentation by Allan of a quite inarticulate client with whom it was difficult to make contact.

**Instructor:** I wonder why you didn't ask him the obvious question about the great gaps in the story of his adolescence. It's as if he jumped from age fourteen to age twenty-two, when he suddenly got married.

**Allan:** I guess it is an obvious question. In fact, it was in my mind when I was taking his history and then I sort of got paralyzed. I pictured all of you sitting here and you [the instructor] sitting at the end of the table. I remembered you said once that direct questions put clients off, that there must be some reason why they don't tell you things, and you shouldn't hit them with questions too directly. I couldn't think of any indirect way to get at it. I would be a lot more direct and less hesitant to get into things that I know need to be gotten into if there weren't somebody to come back and report it to.

Whether the instructor's admonition taken from another context was appropriate to this case is questionable. But Allan does not question it. It is as if "the word" had been spoken and he must follow it obediently.

A second example occurred during a presentation by Ellen of a female client who was twice her age.

**Ellen:**  I found myself talking too much in the middle of the hour, and I didn't know how to stop. It seemed to me that she [the client] looked like you [the instructor]. She had gray hair, you know. Then I thought, what would you say if you heard me going on and on preaching like that? So I just stopped in the middle of a sentence.

**Instructor:**  What happened then?

**Ellen:**  Well, she looked surprised when I stopped, so I tried to finish what I was saying, which was pretty lame. She clammed up and there was an uncomfortable silence. I made another speech that was too long, and when I asked her if she would like to come back for another interview, she said she would think about it. I don't exactly blame her if she doesn't come.

A third example was a part of a case presented by Harriet. The client was a twenty-two-year-old woman employed in a government office.

**Harriet:**  She said she thought perhaps she ought not to come back because talking about these things stirred her up so much. I found myself practically pleading with her to return for at least one more session. My two other clients got their degrees at the end of the first semester and have just left the city. I had thought this one would be more or less steady since she lives and works here, and I didn't want to be left without a client to present. I realized that I wasn't thinking about what was good for her, but just that I needed a client.

**Instructor:**  And that I would eat you up if you didn't have one.

**Harriet:**  I suppose I was feeling something like that. I caught it in time to be able to backtrack and to put forth the issues that concerned the client. Then she said she guessed her worries would come back to bother her anyway if she didn't deal with them, so she is going to return.

**Instructor:**    Congratulations. That was a nice piece of work.

A fourth example came from Bob, presenting a voluble thirty-year-old housewife.

**Bob:**    She talked endlessly and I couldn't get a word in. At the end of the hour I had trouble getting her out of the door in time for my next appointment, and I let her go over time although the next person was waiting for me. I knew I ought to try to find out what she really wanted from therapy, and I hadn't done it yet because it was so hard to keep her to the point and to get a history. I kept thinking that Ellen would say it had all been very superficial, and Doug would say it was unclear and that I seemed to him very confused. I don't know what you would say, Dr. R., except that I shouldn't have let her go over time. But Gail would say I couldn't work with her if I didn't know what she wanted. And everybody would think she had walked over me, so I kept her on and practically shouted at her that I had to find out what her problem was. She got quite annoyed and said she had been telling me about it all this time. So I said, "We have to stop now. Tell me next time so that I can understand it." And I got up and walked out.

It may be that Bob's final intervention was not so untherapeutic as it might seem, but what preceded it was simply a function of his anxiety.

These examples could be multiplied. Some have already been given in earlier chapters. There were surely others that were never reported and still others of which the students themselves were not even aware. Although the instructor appeared to be the main bugaboo, it is clear, especially in the fourth example, that the peer group also exercised considerable power in creating anxiety that stood in the way of therapeutic listening and responding to clients.

The students were, of course, right in assuming that their colleagues and their instructor would criticize their mistakes. Bob, for example, correctly identified the kind of criticism that seminar members tended to make. But the power of these potential criticisms stemmed not simply from the actual experience in the seminar. It stemmed more profoundly from the shadowy figures of long ago that loomed like giants over all of us as small children. They were, of course, primarily parents and teachers. Their power was enormous and, no matter how benevolent they may have been, their not infrequent disapproval was real and frightening. In the third example above, Harriet spoke for the whole group in agreeing that her fears were magnified to proportions that matched those of Hansel and Gretel in their flight from the bad stepparents and in their struggle with the old witch.

It is essential to realize that this seminar was not unusual in this respect. Because these students were learning to be forthright with each other and honest with themselves, the anxiety about this disapproval of persons seen as authority figures emerged more openly than in the usual classroom or supervisory session.

Such anxiety carries with it a good bit of negative feeling. The instructor, who was reasonably well liked on a conscious level by seminar members, readily took on the role of an old witch in the unconscious fantasies of seminar members when they felt, as they sometimes did, like abused children in a fairy tale. Hansel and Gretel were scarcely in any condition to be therapeutic to clients. Neither did they harbor warm feelings toward the old witch whom they shoved into the oven in the happy ending.

The following excerpt from a session near the end of the year indicates that these feelings were present in the seminar, expressed, of course, in a more grownup manner. The excerpt also shows that the antitherapeutic effects of the seminar were not limited to sessions with clients. They appeared to the detriment of the work in the seminar as well. In this context, it cannot be overlooked that the instructor had "real" power, namely, to grade the students and to write good or bad letters of recommendation for them for internships and jobs.

In an individual supervisory interview, Carl had told the instructor that he felt unsupported in the group. Realizing that this was not only Carl's problem but was also a group issue, she urged him to bring up the matter in the next session, and he did.

**Carl:** I have some things on my mind, and I know that Allan has said similar things. I have been feeling very funny in here— very inhibited about making contributions. I sort of felt out of it because the way I have been taught to look at things was so totally different from the way things are being looked at here. I was feeling very inadequate, and what I found myself doing was to make a response and then, if it wasn't picked up by somebody else and if Dr. R. was frowning, I shut up for the rest of the time. I got to the point where I felt that everything was interfering with my contributing and learning. Allan said it too, didn't you?

**Allan:** Yes, and I don't think it had to do with the way you were taught to look at things, either. I felt that something was interfering with the way I would like to function in here. Part of it was wrapped up in making sure I said something for Dr. R.'s benefit, and then the grade was getting in the way too.

**Ellen:** I've been feeling that way, too, off and on—mostly on.

**Carl:** I think one of the worst things I was doing was making excuses for myself, saying that other people have been in the seminar before and they know how things should go and I don't.

**Gail:** I want to respond to that last comment, Carl, about some of us having been here before. It's my third time, and it's never the same; each time is very different. For me, this particular term has changed very dramatically from before because I'm beginning to feel much more a part of the group and I'm getting much more from the experience. But I went through the same kind of thing you're talking about. Maybe it's a phase.

**Bob:** I hear you say you're less anxious, Gail. Well, I'm more anxious. I don't know whether it's a function of me or the group or what. I've been thinking that during the last few times we're not being as effective as we used to be. It could be just a reflection of my own anxiety, but I don't understand the changes.

**Fran:**   They may be different for you than for Gail.

**Instructor:**   I think people's anxiety is bound to go up and down. Within limits, the more anxiety one allows oneself to experience, the more likely one is to learn something. But if people feel their learning is being interfered with—and Carl did—I wish you would bring it up. We could talk about it and see if we could work it through.

**Carl:**   I felt for a while that I was being very silent, very inhibited, as far as speaking out was concerned, and I didn't think I was getting much out of it. Sometimes when I left here I'd be mad as hell because I hadn't said what I was thinking. Maybe I was off the track, but I didn't really think so and I hadn't had a chance to exchange ideas with anyone to find out.

**Gail:**   I think what I've learned is that I say my piece even if people don't agree. But it's taken me quite a while to be comfortable enough to do that.

**Carl:**   I'm hoping that I can feel comfortable enough to do that now that I've brought it up.

**Instructor:**   I hope so too. In fact, maybe you can do it even if you're not comfortable. I'm not sure that being comfortable is the best preparation for learning.

**Harriet:**   I'm never completely comfortable here.

**Ellen:**   I never sleep well the night before I present, so obviously I'm not either.

**Instructor:**   There's a kind of middle ground. If you're too anxious you can't do anything, and if you're not anxious at all, the likelihood of learning is small.

**Fran:**   It just struck me when Ellen said about not sleeping that I'm more anxious here when I'm *not* presenting.

**Bob:**   Yeah, because then you have to critique. That's where you really have to step out on a limb.

**Instructor:** And you can't prepare for that the night before, either.

**Doug:** It has happened to me when I presented that people didn't say anything I could use. They weren't necessarily off base, but either they said things I knew already or I didn't really understand what they meant. Sometimes I talked to people afterward and they confirmed my opinion that most of what was said was showing off for Dr. R. or for each other and it couldn't help much.

**Instructor:** I imagine some of the rest of you feel the same way. What about it?

**Allan:** I suggested to one person the other day that we have a seminar without Dr. R. Maybe we could get some things out that we say to each other afterward but not everyone hears.

**Harriet:** Well, I disagree with that. Dr. R. is not the one who makes things happen here.

**Fran:** Well, she does influence the way we act and what we say and how we say it. And I'm not the only one who is inhibited by it. I like Allan's idea.

**Ellen:** I think it would be a lot of fun to have a meeting by ourselves, but why don't we make it a party, not a seminar?

There has now been ample evidence of the "old witch" role that the instructor plays and the negative feelings that it evokes. Carl has often been "mad as hell." Allan, Fran, Ellen, and others would like to get her off their backs for a change. Harriet wants to deny her importance. The discussion continues.

**Gail:** That's okay, but the real problem is not how nice it would be *without* her, but how to live *with* her. And not only with her, with all the other authorities, too.

Gail demonstrates here that her three semesters in the seminar have truly borne fruit. She has pointed out to the others that the problem cannot be evaded by getting out of this particular seminar or by simply getting rid of the instructor.

The situation of being in relation to a person in authority has to be lived with. The discussion takes a new and deeper turn after her intervention.

**Bob:**  I think you're right. I wish we could just talk about it some more.

**Allan:**  Well, I just wanted to use one session outside to understand what goes on inside.

**Instructor:**  What is going on now, do you think?

**Bob:**  I was thinking that if you [the instructor] were not here, we could really fight it out among ourselves.

**Carl:**  Yes, I'd like a good fight. Let the best man win.

**Ellen:**  Or the best woman.

**Instructor:**  Weren't you fighting anyway? Perhaps in a more subdued way than you would without me here.

**Ellen:**  While we were talking among ourselves, I thought we were each looking at you [the instructor] out of the corners of our eyes and wondering in the back of our minds what you were thinking.

**Instructor:**  Isn't it one of the frustrations and ambiguities of group life that one doesn't know for sure or 100 percent what other people are thinking?

**Doug:**  It would be dull if we did.

**Carl:**  I guess I tend to assume that people are not thinking very good thoughts about me—especially when I have presented and people point out that I have made an error. That puts me lower on the totem pole. What makes me mad is that other people talk down at me to elevate themselves and their position in the seminar and to keep me down.

**Bob:**  It's the old thing about competition again. Who's the best therapist?

**Gail:**  And who is Dr. R.'s favorite?—which might not be the same thing.

**Doug:** Aren't we all trying to compete for that position, the favorite child position?

**Harriet:** I don't think that there is any one favorite child here.

**Ellen:** I'm very tuned into the support people get, mainly from Dr. R. When one of us does not get support from her, then that person is clearly not favored.

**Instructor:** Are you sure? I think one thing you're missing is that lack of support by me might be a great compliment.

**Ellen:** I hadn't thought of it that way. I suppose we do feel sometimes like a bunch of cripples who can't stand up by ourselves.

**Allan:** When you see somebody else getting supported, it seems as though it would feel nice.

**Carl:** It's not so much support to help me to stand up that I want. I want more pats on the back. I'd like Dr. R. to tell me, "That was a marvelous job you did with your client."

**Instructor:** I have been thinking that we don't exploit sufficiently the situations in which things are going well. We concentrate a lot on the places where things are going badly.

**Allan:** Well, it makes sense to use the seminar as a place to bring problems. You don't go to take lessons from a tennis pro when you're playing very well.

**Gail:** Yes, but when you watch a good player it can improve your own game. I'd like to hear more of situations that are handled skillfully. I think I could learn from that.

**Fran:** You know, I think I avoided bringing in some of the best work I did for fear that people would think I was bragging or trying to be one up.

**Bob:** I think I did that too. It was a way to avoid the competition, supposedly, but of course it didn't.

**Fran:** Do you think we'll ever get over it, the competition, I mean?

**Instructor:**   No, I don't, not until you become saints or something.

**Ellen:**   But sometimes we seem to forget it and those are the best times.

**Carl:**   It could happen that there are more and more of those times. It is better right now, for me anyway.

**Instructor:**   So long as you don't expect it to stay that way.

**Gail:**   I guess it's something you have to lose and get back over and over again.

Two elements in the competition among group members have been touched on in this discussion: the question of who would be the strongest and most antiauthority leader who would be willing to take on the instructor, and the question of who would be the instructor's favorite.* Both of these issues might have been emphasized if this had been a self-study or therapy group. They were present in the seminar but, as the instructor said, in subdued form. As mature young people engaged in serious study, the students consciously wanted to use the instructor as a teacher and resource person, not as an adversary to be overthrown or a parent to take care of them. But less consciously, as in all groups, the elements of adolescent rebellion and childish dependency were present and active. Occasionally it became important to air these subterranean

---

*The reader familiar with Bion's concepts will recognize in these two questions aspects of the two basic assumptions: fight and dependency. Both basic assumptions can contribute to the work group, but can also, if they predominate, interfere with its function. (Cf. *Experiences in Groups*, by Wilfred Bion, Basic Books, 1966. Cf. also "The Work of Wilfred R. Bion on Groups," in *Psychiatry*, 1970, 33: 56-66, by M. J. Rioch.) The flight group was also sometimes in evidence when the group engaged in chitchat or irrelevant discussion. This was infrequent, however, and there are no extended examples of it in this book, since such excerpts would not be particularly enlightening to readers. The pairing group also occurred from time to time. Pairing in the service of work can be found, for example, in the first presentation in Chapter Seven and also in the present chapter, when Allan supports Carl.

processes when they interfered with the optimal functioning of the group. Then they could be forgotten again. As Ellen pointed out, the best times were those when these interferences had gone back into their subterranean caves and been forgotten or when they fed into the task of the group as dedication to independent and excellent work. The antitherapeutic aspects of supervision in the training of therapists need to be recognized. If they are not denied, their interference with clinical work can be minimized and the dynamic forces behind them can be employed in the service of the task.

# CHAPTER 13

# CONCLUDING COMMENTS

The beginning psychotherapist who takes his work seriously is in a truly difficult situation. He or she is faced not only with two mainstreams of psychological thought that he must integrate, or between which he must choose, but he is bombarded on all sides by a thousand and one new approaches to psychological problems, each one stridently claiming to be more effective than the one before. It is scarcely possible for him to do his daily work and keep up even with their names. But this is not the worst of his troubles. He is no doubt struggling with all the normal and sometimes neurotic problems of a young person who has not yet established himself in this uncertain society. At the same time he believes he is expected to guide others, often older than he is, who are struggling with the same problems in more aggravated form. His own life experience is limited, and he is probably more than a little baffled in his search for a meaningful place in the world on which to stand. But he must appear to his professors and his fellow students to be quite in command of the situation and to know the answers as well as any of them. As Dr. Johnson said of his dog, it is not so surprising that he cannot walk easily on two feet as that he can walk on two feet at all.

One response to this situation can sometimes be observed in clinical case presentations. The clinician reports the neurotic, defensive patterns of his client with a superior attitude of "How on earth can he be so foolish" (or "so naive" or "so stupid")? If anyone, particularly an instructor, calls attention to this attitude, it is quickly denied or covered over—but not before the underlying uncertainty has been betrayed about how to respond to the client's dilemma, which, after all, is not so different from the clinician's own dilemma.

At age twenty-five it is not unreasonable to be in conflict and turmoil, to be uncertain of one's direction, and to be anxious about one's interpersonal relationships as well as about one's work. In fact, it is not unreasonable at any age. But there is an unspoken demand upon students to act as if they were wise men who have found the truth, when the fact is that they are searching in the wilderness for small glimmers of light.

It is now fairly commonly accepted that insight in psychotherapy is not enough. Tracing the client's neurotic behavior to its origins in childhood is an interesting occupation, and it sometimes frees a person from the burdens of the past. More often, it leaves both client and therapist with a frustrated sense of "I know all that, but it doesn't change anything." Just how and when the emotional experience that does bring about change can occur is not at all well understood and is still less prescribable. All the simple cookbook recipes that tell the student "how to do it" have a function in providing him with resting places in the tangle of conflicting values and conflicting claims that surround all of us in this last quarter of the twentieth century. Beginning therapists have to take their courage in their hands to admit how frequently they do not know what they are doing. Actually, experienced people, too, conceal their uncertainties a large part of the time. Among friends it can be confessed that the ultimate questions of psychotherapy are not so easy to answer. Perhaps they are not answerable at all.

It is a great relief to have the kind of respite from uncertainty that behavior therapy provides. The client presents a limited problem. The therapist prescribes a definite procedure for its alleviation. Many instructors start off by being present in the interview and modeling what to do. The student masters the technique by imitation. He learns a relatively uncomplicated theory that seems to fit with common sense.

This brief description obviously oversimplifies, in the interest of highlighting the predicament created by the client's vague but persistent complaints when they are presented to an ambitious young student who is trying to look like a psychotherapist dealing with psychodynamic conflicts. "I am depressed," the client says; or "I feel tense, anxious, worried. I've felt this way for a long time, maybe all my life. I don't know why, but I want to get at the root of it." And the student himself is feeling tense, anxious, worried, without being able to get at the root of it. For the root of it is the human condition, aggravated by threats of atomic war, overpopulation, and the lack of binding traditions.

The predicament of the student in this situation is matched by that of his teacher. Let us assume that the teacher is mature, stable, well established in career and family, and firmly grounded in the theory and practice of psychodynamic or analytic psychotherapy. These assumptions will, of course, rightly raise the skeptical eyebrows of student readers. But let us make them for the sake of simplifying the argument. How and what shall this enviable being teach? He can, of course, teach psychoanalytic theory, with all its variations and ramifications. But then what? His students bring him living people who rarely match the ones in the literature. What shall he do? If this book has served its purpose well, it will not have provided solutions to this problem. It will, however, have underlined the difficulties and dangers in clinical teaching. In any school, university, or other teaching and learning institution, the illusion dies hard that the staff knows the answers. Sometimes the staff itself shares this illusion. The teaching of psychotherapy contains the paradox that the supervisor has something to teach but the student must learn it for himself.

Supervision of psychodynamic psychotherapy can be classified in three main categories, one of which approximates the "I'll show you how to do it" kind that was mentioned earlier in describing behavior therapy. In this kind of supervision, the teacher tells the student what he would do if *he* were treating the particular client. But, alas, there are at least two pitfalls in this approach. One lies in the fact that the teacher is telling the student what he *would* have done in the situation that occurred last week. Unhappily, this situation may not be reproduced when the student sees the client the following week. Of course, the same pattern may recur, and the student may be faced with a situation similar to the one his supervisor advised him about. But then we find the second pitfall. The student is all too prone to take the instructor literally. He will say the same words, but at the wrong moment, or with the wrong tone of voice, or with some variation that circumvents the teacher's intention. More often than not, there is an unconscious motivation here to prove the teacher a fool. Chapter Twelve has elaborated on this. But even if conscious and unconscious motivations are pure, the student, being a different person from the teacher, is almost bound to put a different note in his voice than the one that would have worked well for the teacher.

The second kind of supervision does not attempt to tell the student how to do it but tries to help by explaining the client more fully than the student has understood him. This can be done brilliantly by supervisors who have had years of clinical experience. At its best, it provides the student who can listen with a better map of the territory that he is exploring, a more

faithful portrait of the physiognomy that he is trying to see by
the unsteady candlelight that is the only illumination allowed
by the client. The student is often appropriately grateful for
this help. The difficulty with this kind of teaching is that it can
easily make for greater distance between the student and his
client, as well as between the supervisor and the student. The
latter comes to see his client as a thing to be explored, an object
to be perceived more clearly. If he assimilates the wisdom of his
supervisor, he becomes more penetrating in his insights, more
knowledgeable in his theoretical foundations. Sometimes he
also becomes more damaging by virtue of the increased sharp-
ness of his instruments. He tries to outdo his supervisor in the
brilliance of his dynamic formulations and to be ready for his
next supervisory session with a barrage of articulate questions
and answers.

A third kind of supervision attempts to work with the
student's anxieties and his defenses against them. By and large,
it is this kind that has been presented in the excerpts included
in this book, although the first two kinds have made occasional
appearances as well. When this third kind is successful, it
enables the student to find his own way a little better than he
had before. It enables him to use his own capacities, both intellectual and emotional, in forming a therapeutic alliance with his
client without the encumbrance of defensive maneuvers. But
this is an ideal that is by no means always attained. And the
pitfalls of this kind of supervision are serious. Some of them
have been indicated in Chapter Eight on Failures and in Chapter
Twelve on The Antitherapeutic Aspects of the Seminar. There is
another kind of danger that did not occur in this group because
the members were all approximately on a par with each other in
experience and competence. They had high regard for each
other's abilities. Their weaknesses could be both tolerated and
criticized in an atmosphere of mutual respect. This situation
does not always obtain. One member of a group who fails to
earn a necessary minimum of esteem from his fellows can
greatly impair the work of the total group. It is possible that a
skillful group therapist could manage or alleviate this problem.
But this seminar had made it a matter of principle not to do
more than occasionally dip into the territory of group therapy.

Thus, although an unaccepted member can be "handled" and tolerated, the fact of his presence is a disadvantage to the group. It is even more of a disadvantage to him personally. Unless he is extraordinarily insensitive, he will be aware of the lack of respect that the others have for him. He may respond to this with grandiose, paranoid fantasies, especially if the group has sensed a lack of integrity in him. More often he responds by developing feelings of inferiority that interfere with the quality of his work, so that it becomes even worse than it was to begin with. Thus, supervision of the third type is fraught with dangers for the individual and difficulties for the supervisor and the group.

The question has to be raised whether the risk is worth the candle. Do the students learn enough to make it worth the potential and occasionally actual damage to an individual? Teachers of psychotherapy have no reliable way of measuring what their students have learned. They rely upon impressions and anecdotes, most of which are supplied by the very students whose learning they are trying to evaluate. The students themselves can only estimate what have been contributing factors in their development as therapists. The teacher who is in despair at not being able to communicate anything of value to a particular student may the next day become exaggeratedly cheered by evidence of improved therapeutic skill. The reverse occurs equally often.

There is no way to escape the fact that in doing psychotherapy, as well as in teaching it, we are not really able to count the cost or measure the results, although we engage in counting and measuring to satisfy the demands of insurance companies and the need to be "scientific." But the truth is that we are performing an act of faith—faith in our clients, or patients if we prefer to call them that, and faith in our students. It does not really matter that this is occasionally misplaced or that we fail more than once in spite of experience and skill. Like other kinds of faith, this one persists although it is based on things unseen and unheard. Essentially, it is faith in the value of truth, not so much truth with a capital T that would reveal to us the nature of ultimate reality, but truth as the opposite of the small daily self-deceptions or the large paranoid delusions that destroy men's respect for themselves and for each other.

# INDEX